"Marla is writing the deconstruction n
Cutting out all the extra words we wa
Marla goes straight for the guts. I nev
looping thoughts and to invite me to sit with my own grief, pain, anger, and—
surprisingly—my joy at breaking free. This is a book for anyone in the thick of
deconstruction. Marla will be a good, creative, and curious friend on your own
journey to healing."

D. L. Mayfield, author of *Unruly Saint: Dorothy Day's Radical
Vision and its Challenge for our Times*

"An unrelenting love letter to the deconstructing exvangelical in all of us, *jaded*
kicks your ass in all the ways you never knew you needed. Marla's collection
of salty and sweet, diverse-drenched poems delivers punch after punch of inclu-
sion, truth, and authentic calls for change. Read this book—it will do your heart,
mind, and backside good."

Stacey Chomiak, author and illustrator of *Still Stace: My Gay
Christian Coming-of-Age Story*

"Marla Taviano's latest collection of poetry holds the beauty of her uncluttered
and unencumbered way with words. In *jaded*, she sees the thing but allows the
reader to see what she sees without intruding or leading, and without assuming.
For instance, in her poem 'ten years ago' the thoughts are loud and profound
while the lyricism of the poem is still and quiet—as if waiting for us to take a
synchronized breath with the poet. A beautiful invitation is offered here."

Marcie Alvis Walker, *Black Coffee with White Friends*
and author of *Everybody Come Alive*

"*Jaded* follows Marla's first collection of poems on deconstructing white evangelicalism. She says the soft part LOUD, offering much-needed language for
those in the wilderness trying to make sense of faith in the bid toward wholeness."

Rohadi Nagassar, author of *When We Belong* and host
of the *Faith in a Fresh Vibe* podcast

"Poetry exposes the wound, names the wound, and heals the wound—with love.
Poetry also advocates for the wound and speaks the truth about the wound. This
is how I see Marla's poetry. She is a gifted writer whose book, *jaded*, is neces-
sary for all who are on the path of liberation from toxic white supremacy culture
and colonization. May all who read *jaded* feel seen, heard, and understood."

Tasha Hunter, author of *What Children Remember* and host
of the *When We Speak* podcast

jaded

jaded

a poetic reckoning with
white evangelical christian indoctrination

marla taviano

lakedrivebooks.com

Lake Drive Books
6757 Cascade Road SE, 162
Grand Rapids, MI 49546

info@lakedrivebooks.com
lakedrivebooks.com
@lakedrivebooks

Publishing books that help you heal, grow, and discover.

Paperback ISBN: 978-1-957687-16-2
eBook ISBN: 978-1-957687-17-9

Library of Congress Control Number: 2022950387

Gorgeous cover art and design by Olivia Taviano

dedication

to each reader-friend

picking up pieces
of life and faith

and figuring out
how to heal and
move forward

I believe in you
I'm rooting for you

we've got this

feel free to use the
white space in this book

to process your
thoughts and feelings

via words or sketches
as you read

I left lots of it
just for you

contents

jaded

adjective: tired, bored
or lacking enthusiasm

typically after having had
too much of something

made cynical by experience
and over it already

but also: can't
seem to let it go

welcome

hi friend

if you haven't read my book
unbelieve, you need to

if you have and liked it
but wished it would have

been a little spicier
you'll love *jaded*

if *unbelieve* made you cringe
you might want to

gently lay this book down
and back away for a bit

just so you know

jaded is
unbelieve's
bitchy
little
sister

2.5 stars!

"Minor praise for Marla Taviano
who lays it all out in her book, *unbelieve.*"

—S. R.

I was scrolling Instagram
in a dream
and saw this "review"
of my book

I was pleasantly surprised
because she's not a fan of me
in real life

coming from her,
minor praise is
quite the compliment

scratch that

unbelieve (sort of) ended
with wings and freedom

a lilting, happy, hopeful
where do I go from here?

the plan was to move
on to a second book

working title: *more*

where I'd share my bigger,
lovelier, more expansive

thoughts about god and
spirituality and the world

but *jaded* wouldn't leave
me the hell alone

turns out (a haiku)

I have a whole lot
more to get off my chest so
here we fucking go

fuck yeah

"Sorry for all the swears
but I'm a recovering

Good Religious Girl

and it's an important
part of my recovery!"

—**D. L. Mayfield**

even though...

I had largely untangled myself from
the lies and beliefs, they went

deep / my insides wouldn't let my
outsides write that expansive book

yet / I still had work to do to help
us get free / I long for a beautiful

world beyond white evangelical
christianity but I feel a pull to get

people out / partly because I care
about them, mostly because I care

about people they're harming / I
harmed people too and have wrongs

to right/write as I move into freedom
so here is my labor of anger and love

more is still to come

no shame / just do better

ignorant, often used as an
insult, actually means *lacking*

knowledge or awareness which
can be remedied with a desire

and effort to learn / it's a whole
other thing to be willfully stubborn

refusing to hear uncomfortable
truths / I'm not here to shame you

or even get you to *unbelieve*
exactly like I do / I want us to

think for ourselves, not just swallow
what we've been told / let's

become un-ignorant of injustice
and how we all perpetuate it

whether we mean to or not / let's
move from unknowing to knowing

then from knowing to taking
action to stop the harm

bite me

it's tempting to tamp down
my emotion

to make it more palatable
easier to swallow

don't want to come across
as angry and bitter

but I *am* those things

I'm also healing and happy
I'm a lover and a fighter

both/and

and I'm not as worried about
anyone's palate these days

you can read another poet
if you're craving something

sweet

hi, god / *it's me, mara*

"Don't call me Naomi," she told them, "Call
me Mara [Marla], because the Almighty
has made my life very bitter." (Ruth 1:20)

once upon a time
my mother named me
Marla Rachelle
after the bible's
Mary and Rachel

Marla means motherly
she told me, smiling

but I found out otherwise
when my ex's grandmother
bought me a photo frame
with a watercolor print

Marla in fancy font
BITTER in bold caps

I was offended then
but I'm smiling now

and taking bitter back

dumpster fire

so much for "getting things out of my
system" when shit keeps getting worse

evangelical christians cause more harm
become more toxic / more people suffer

I try to write this damn book and every
damn day another shooting, another

hard-fought-for law overturned, another
human right stripped away, another white

person bitching about a Black mermaid
jaded isn't a strong enough word for how

I feel / "I want to write rage but all that
comes is sadness," Audre Lorde once

said / I know that sadness but today I
want to write rage and so I do

like the shape of a book

"I started teaching myself
to contort my rage
into more valuable shapes;
it doesn't disappear that way,
just works for you
instead of against you."

—**Nafissa Thompson-Spires**

holy anger liberates

as a white woman,
the deepest rage is
not mine to feel

white people have long
demonized Black anger,
Cole Arthur Riley says

anger is never holier than
when it acts in defense
of another being's dignity

when righteous anger
swells, so does justice

Black rage is a gift
I want to honor

fierce love

While I've retreated from some
of what the church has taught—

women are inferior, queer people are sinners,
white people are predestined to rule the world,

non-Christians are doomed to hell—
I've doubled down on my belief in love.

It's my North Star.

—Rev. Dr. Jacqui Lewis

clapping my hands
yes / this / is / it

love

not walking away
not anger and hate
not bitter rage

love
period.

but first
just a weeeeee bit of
jadedness

16

indoctrination

ten years ago

time for our nightly bedtime story
from *The Jesus Storybook Bible*

"Abraham sacrifices Isaac"

my 10-year-old sees
the page before I begin

Ava: *oh no!*
I don't like this one!
It's so scary!
Mom, would you ever do that?

me: *if god told me to*

Ava: *well do it on Livi or Nina*

imagine

slaughtering your child on an altar
because god told you to or else

what in the actual *hell*?

the bible is full of violent stories
that are not kid-appropriate

and most adults can't really
be trusted with them either

I obviously couldn't (sheesh)
and now I recognize the sad sad

truth / my flippant answer to my
precious daughter was just me

desperately trying to prove to
god that I'd pick him over my

kids so he would never ask me
to willingly give them up

I used to think

*gay people can't take the rainbow and
buddhists can't take white elephants*

those are god's

well how about evangelical christians
can't take god? / god is everyone's

and what kind of god kills almost
every creature on the planet, then

casually says *this was just a one and
done okay? / seriously, I promise*

see, here's a rainbow

far-fetched

can someone explain to me
why I should believe that a

snake really talked and so did
an ass (the donkey kind) and

Noah's family survived an
actual worldwide flood and

Jonah lived in a fish's belly
for three whole days and god

made woman from man's rib
and the world in 7 days but

other religions' fantastical
stories are nothing but myths?

James 2:18-20

the bible *literally* says
that what you believe

doesn't matter an ounce if
your deeds don't match up

AND YOUR DEEDS DON'T
MATCH UP DAMN IT

skitsnack

once you've studied another
language you realize how

impossible it is to translate
exactly precisely without

losing any meaning or context
along the way / that fact alone

is enough to show me that
taking the bible "literally"

while reading it in English
is cazzate / mierda / foutèz

bullshit

speaking of feces

do the evangelical cussing police
know about the word *skubalon*

Paul uses in Philippians 3:8? / it's
translated as *dung* or *garbage*

in English bibles but it's more
vulgar than that / if you want to

take the bible *literally* you've
gotta translate *skubalon* as *shit*

(purposely) lost in translation

righteousness clearly means *personal
piety and holiness*, I thought / but

Obery M. Hendricks Jr. says righteousness
(*tzedekah*) is correctly translated as

doing right by others / *acting with
justice* / *loving your neighbor*

HOLD UP

are you saying that
righteousness = social justice?

yes and the bible says it too

one way to get out of actually
obeying the bible is to take it

literally

in a language it wasn't
even written in

why the Paul fetish?

90% of the verses you stab people with
are Paul's words, not Christ's / are you

a christian or a Paulian? / which guy did
you ask into your heart? / plus also?

Paul's letters weren't written to us / and
what did the letters *to* him even say?

you pluck random Paulisms from a bible
you say is literal while ignoring all the

prophets (and Jesus) and call yourself
a christian, so I can pull out the love

and justice verses and call myself one
too / it's why I can't give up on the

bible yet / there's a lot of shit in there
that lines up with my love ethic / too bad

none of our cherry-picking overlaps

Darth Paul

I wish the Paul-lovers would quote
the verses where he loses his cool

and wants to kick people in the nuts
(wants them to *remove their own*

testicles, rather, because they insist
on a literal bible) / don't believe me?

see Galatians 5:12 where he's pissed
at certain disciples who insist on

circumcision for everyone / Paul
wishes the agitators would go all

the way and castrate themselves
I've never felt so close to the dude

look at us both mad at theobros
who demand that law trumps love

I have to say that Paul's dark side
is one I can actually get behind

it's personal

it's not a religion
it's a relationship
they told me

well, that sure is a hell
of a lot of rules for a
relationship

ridiculous

here's a 1978 World Book
Encyclopedia set
you're set for life

we wouldn't dream of telling our kids
everything you will ever need to know
about the world is in this one book

or even

everything you will ever need to know
about stars or *dolphins* or *ice cream*
or *plants* or *cars* or *Chicago*

but everything there is to know
about *god*
is in this *one book*?

yeah no / how could

everything there is to know
about god
be in this *one book*?

fire insurance

does it count if
I only say

the sinner's prayer

because I'm scared
to burn in hell?

groom groom

it's pretty smart to indoctrinate
kiddos from a tiny age, all while

being told by "experts" that you're
"growing them god's way" / get

into their sweet malleable brains
long before they fully develop and

it's free sailing for a good while

this practice is insidious and I
absolutely did it / thought it made

me a good mom / I played right into
their hands and I'm so glad my kids

got out before I messed them up bad
instead of just messing them up a

probably-fixable medium amount

hiding god's word in your heart

I once read that

twelve to twenty years of stupefying
memorization drills weakens
the hardiest intellects

and *light bulb*

two words: *scripture memory*

what could possibly be the point of
memorizing huge chunks, even whole

chapters of scripture except to use up
valuable brain space and weaken and

indoctrinate your once-hardy intellect?

the lifelong drill

we're right / they're wrong
we're right / they're wrong
we're right / they're wrong
we're right / they're wrong
we're right / they're wrong
we're right / they're wrong
we're right / they're wrong
we're right / they're wrong
we're right / they're wrong
we're right / they're wrong
we're right / they're wrong
we're right / they're wrong

wait
what if it's
the other way
around?

read the room

some theorists say *you cannot stretch*
more than one step above your own

level of consciousness, and that is
on a good day / most of us are only

willing to call into question 5% of our
present information at a time and we

can save ourselves a lot of distress by
knowing when / where / to whom / how

to talk about spiritually mature things

so… Facebook? / lol no

zealous

born again with a twist

people came to our church
when I was a kid and shared

their dramatic *testimony* of how
bad they were and how god

saved them later in life from
drugs and sex and rock-n-roll

I was such a good girl, got
saved when I was three and

stayed on the straight and
narrow for decades

what a boring *testimony*

who knew god would save me
(or maybe I saved myself?)

later in life from toxic patriarchal
white supremacist religion

and give me that thrilling
testimony I'd always envied

maybe you were never saved

so you've walked away from god
they look down their noses at me

maybe you never had a personal
relationship with him after all

um, tell that to my 62 journals
where I wrote to the lord with

intense fervor and passion and
miles of jargon and hyperboles

every freaking day for 20+ years

sounds pretty damn serious and
really super personal to me

(although now it feels like I was
writing to an imaginary pen pal)

bleeding heart

opening my journals feels
like reopening old wounds

both the ones inflicted
on me and the ones I

caused / I know people
who have burned theirs

but I need to read mine
to dive deep into my past

to see which harmful
beliefs led me here and

which ones I'm still
clinging to and how I'm

going to get all the dang
way free / keeping a

tourniquet handy just in
case it gets messy

worthless

I didn't make it two
pages before I realized

just how much toxic
shit I believed

I thought I was a
wretch, that god was

punishing me
keeping us poor

so we'd be forced
to rely on him

I was too needy
too selfish

undeserving
not a good soldier

absolute trash
without god

self-brainwashing mechanism

back in the day god fit neatly inside
my journal / he was *Dear Lord* like

my mama taught me / calm and quiet
and liked me best when I sat quietly

before him with my bible and journal
lots of humble prayer / everything good

in my life was because of him / all the
bad was satan's fault / no credit went to

me, the lowly wretched worm / I used
journaling to cement beliefs I struggled

with, like submitting to my husband
so much repetition of wrong, harmful

ideas wore the grooves deeper, faster
what a dangerous daily habit for a girl

with an already toxic theology

take my day and make it yours

that was my morning prayer
for years and years and years

ugh I want my days back

sad tales of a former eschatology junkie

god this is embarrassing but I ate up all
that apocalyptic pre-tribulation stuff / I

thought my deconstruction started with
caring for the poor but my journals say it

began with me questioning if the rapture
is real and which trib's the best trib / I even

got roped into writing a book proposal:
A Woman's Guide to the End of the World

by my agent as publishers' eyes rolled
I fired him and he reps NYT bestsellers

now / am I still bitter? / as it all comes
flooding back to me, yeah / joke's on me

I got left behind in more ways than one

Team Marla or Team Paul?

here's why you should listen to me, Paul said

*circumcised on the eighth day / tribe of
Benjamin / Hebrew of Hebrews / as to the
law, a Pharisee / a persecutor of the church /
as to righteousness under the law, blameless*

hey Paul I see your faultless acquiescence
and severed foreskin and raise you:

*missions conference attendee / "serving my
master" badge earner / camp counselor /
nursery worker / vacation bible school
teacher / Sunday school teacher / preacher /
clown ministry / campus crusader for christ /
young life leader / ministry founder / missionary*

were you ever a *christian clown*, Paul?
didn't think so

and I know you wrote long
letters to house churches

but I wrote entire *books* helping
wives submit to their husbands

so let's put this to a vote

speech! speech!

I graduated co-valedictorian at my
public high school and gave this address:

*I've spent an awful lot of time these
past four years worrying about A's*

*and now... I'd like to jump down the
grading scale... and talk about F's*

*3 F's in particular—faith, future, friends
the first F is my faith in Jesus Christ*

*I didn't always share my faith with
my classmates like I wish I would've*

*I had many opportunities, but I was
usually too afraid / fortunately today*

*I've been given one more chance
I don't want to preach a sermon . . .*

I went on to preach a fucking sermon
so much arrogance in those young bones

asking forgiveness 2.5 decades too late

I asked for it

god use me
for your purposes
use me
for your glory
use me
for your kingdom
not my will
but thine
use me
take everything
out of me
I just want
to be used
by you
used
and abused
taken advantage of
left hanging
out to dry
all used up
until there's
nothing left
what an honor
and a privilege
to be used
used
used

so odd

I asked god to use me
and that's exactly what

god did except for some
reason god looked a lot

like all the men in power
in my church/home/life

scare tactics

the threat of hell

is simply
how you
keep
people
in your
cult

curiosity killed the cult

cult (loosely defined) is
unquestioningly doing things

on earth because all that matters
is what happens after death

I'm not ever doing anything
unquestioningly again

I'll ask questions and dig
deeper and study history

and uncover secrets and
demand proof and be

oh-so-very curious and never
ever settle for "god said so"

ever ever ever again

C+ god

in his landmark book *Love Wins*
Rob Bell quotes 1 Timothy 2

God wants all people to be saved

sooo… does god get what god
wants? he asks / is god great

enough to accomplish what he
says he wants to do? / which is it—

all people will be saved / or the
almighty god doesn't get what

he wants? / is god just kind of
great, medium great, sometimes

great, not totally great? / *how does
eternal torment bring God glory?*

Rob and I want to know

sorry about the hell

when Rachel Held Evans said she once
believed that the piles of suitcases and

bags of human hair at the holocaust
museum represented thousands of people

burning in eternal torment in hell because
they were jewish, not christian, I wanted

to throw up / are the millions of people
who have never been exposed to

christianity doomed to hell? / "seekers"
used to ask me how this is fair or right

I'd say, *I know it sounds harsh, but we
have to trust god* / and oh my god, could

I have spiritual-bypassed any harder?

heaven help me

I'm not scared of death / I'm scared
of the unfathomable sadness that

comes with it / for me or the people
I leave behind / I want to know I'll see

my kids again / *I want an afterlife damn it*

I get why heaven is so comforting but
why do christians need hell so badly?

what does it say about my heart if the
thought of most of humanity suffering

in eternal torment brings me comfort?

that face when

you come to the
conclusion that

not only is there
no hell

but
white
evangelical
christianity

is the hell

shaking in its boots

"Institutional Christianity seems
fearful of inquiry,
fearful of freedom,
fearful of knowledge—

indeed, fearful of anything
except its own repetitious propaganda,
which has its origins in a world
that none of us any longer inhabits.

The Church historically has been
willing to criticize,
marginalize, or even expel
its most creative thinkers."

—Bishop John Shelby Spong

smooth as silk

the world will try to
ensnare you in evils
and lies, you warned

and that whole time
you had me strung up
in a web of evils and lies
you had disguised as truth

just like a spider paralyzing
her prey and wrapping
it up in a deadly
cocoon of beautiful
compressing silk

before she injects it
with venom and crushes
its body with her fangs
and liquefies it with
her digestive juices

just like that

my soul to keep

fear is a tactic used by
evangelical christianity to

keep you from exploring
your questions and doubts

keep you from leaving
keep you toeing the line

when you open your eyes
step into the unknown

you see that the monster in
the corner is just a shadow

you meet muslims and see
they're good people

you meet gay people and
their "agenda" isn't scary

you meet atheists who
are fun and kind

love is dangerous because
it casts out fear

oh my god

god's butt

can you sing me the song about
the king and the rear end?

she asks me in that sweet but
raspy little 5-year-old voice

I don't know a song about a
king and a rear end, I laugh

yes you do, she insists and I wrack
my brain and finally it hits me

and I somehow keep a very straight
and solemn face as I begin to sing

the lyrics to "i love you lord and I
lift my voice" which copyright laws

say I cannot include in a book so you
will have to google them but there is

most definitely something about god
as *king* and how the singer would like

my voice to sound sweet in

your rear

delicious confession

I love love love
saying *oh my god*
because for so long

I was tricked into
believing it was
a terrible sin

turns out
it's barely even
a medium sin

the logic

you are loved by god and
created in his image

and

a worthless piece of shit
who is nothing without him

let me make…

some wretched creatures
who don't deserve me
and desperately need me

and who I'll burn in hell
if they don't worship me

and also make sure
everyone thinks
they have free will

and I'll call myself
a loving god

sound good?
do we like this plan?
not that it matters

I'm in charge here
not you

let me get this straight

if I get blessings
because I was living right
that's god's *favor*

if I get shit
because I was bad
that's god's *obligation*

if I get shit
but I was living right,
that's god's *testing*

so no matter what
god can't lose and has
it made in the shade

this isn't mix and match

my mom prayed for my future
husband upon my exit from the

womb / his mom got pregnant
with him four months later / I

used to tell the story of how my
mother-in-law was headed for

an abortion clinic and something
stopped her / my mama's prayers?

too bad my mama's prayers didn't
stop that baby from growing up

to cheat on me / divorce me / and
abandon his daughters / shall we

give god credit for one but not
blame for the other? / not today

maxed out

god gets
credit for this
and
credit for that
and more
and more
credit

all
all
all

the credit

please pass me
the scissors
and watch me
cut this card
into pieces

I thank, just not god

I'm all about an attitude of
gratitude but I can just say I'm

thankful, grateful / I don't need
to say *thank you, god, for this*

brief respite in an otherwise shitty
month that of course isn't your

fault at all / I only invoke your
name when you put my fave frozen

pizza on sale, not when things go
horribly terribly hurtfully wrong

September 15, 2011

me to Ava (9): why do you think god
is blessing us so stinking much today?

Ava: probably because he felt
so bad for us about yesterday

hand of god

praise you
gracious god
for protecting me
and my family

by moving
that hurricane
out of the path
of my home

the quiet part:
and into someone else's

just as good

give your burdens to god
cast your cares upon him

or you can just set them
down on that bench

almighty all-powerful runner-up god

if there's only one true god then
who is all the "spiritual warfare"

against? / *satan and his demons*
but isn't god omnipotent? / *of course*

yet he still has to fight demons?
yes / and he doesn't defeat them?

he does / but bad stuff still happens?
yeah because of free will / sooo...

god lets satan win at torture and
destroying lives? / *yes* / why doesn't

god just kill satan? / *because free will* /
but he kills tons of people in the bible

for minor infractions / *god's ways are*

higher than ours / oh... got it, except
I don't really got it at all and I'm

pretty sure you don't got it either

Romans 8:28

I can maybe believe
there's a "reason"

I was fired
got a rejection letter
my plan failed
car broke down
even my husband left me

each of those could possibly
lead to something bigger
brighter better than I can see
right now in my pain

if that's what you mean by
a "reason"

but don't you dare
tell my friends there's
a "reason"

their daughter died
or that her death will work
together for good in the end or
that it was god's will

to hell with that bullshit

I pity the fool

"Poor humankind,
to have invented
the gods,
and thrown in
a bad temper
as well!"

—Lucretius

over / lord

I took *lord* out of my vocabulary
in light of all those awful journal

entries / then I heard Alice Walker
say *the word Lord is so man-derived,*

so oppressively classist, that its effect
is to stifle the urge to worship, rather

than stimulate it and now
I don't like it even more

did I get this right?

we were enslaved to sin and
headed for hell

when Jesus swooped in
and saved us

paid a debt so big
we could never repay him

so we're technically free
but enslaved to him for life

so we're like...
indentured servants for Jesus?

feels like a full-time job

I'm not *making up my own god*
I'm trying to figure out who god

really truly is after being
lied to my whole life

disability justice

full of holes

years ago I read a book called *The
Hole in Our Gospel* and discovered

that loving the poor was a missing
piece in my faith journey / I just read

a book called *My Body Is Not a Prayer
Request* and discovered another gaping

hole—*disability justice*—and I'm
going to try to make up for it now

glaring omission

reading through
journal
after journal
after journal
and

nothing anywhere
about racism
or whiteness
or queerness
or disability

or anything else
that didn't directly
affect me

I never ever
had to think
about it
at all

not
one
single
time

don't dance around disability

disabled people are not a monolith
and each individual is free to identify
themselves in whatever way they wish

whenever possible, ask people to
share their preferred terminology,
Emily Ladau suggests

well-meaning euphemisms fall flat,
she says—*differently abled, special needs,*
handi-capable, physically challenged

disabled is not a dirty word, writes
Keah Brown, *I want the world to*
know that I am disabled and proud

I am not a euphemism or a metaphor.
I am disabled, Amy Kenny says,

my disabled body is made
of the same stuff as stars

past the expiration date

we can choose violence
with our words sometimes
without even realizing it

the word "lame"
means unable to walk
without difficulty

but we use it to mean
disappointing/pathetic/dull
never in a positive context

this is hurtful to our
disabled siblings and it's
past time to toss it in the trash

let's learn about hurtful slurs
and expand our vocabulary
in a way that honors everyone

no more disability metaphors

language is a repository for
our biases, Amy Kenny writes

when we use disability as a metaphor
for weakness, we perpetuate ableism

paralyzed by fear
she used the excuse as a *crutch*
I was *blind* to the way I hurt her
his suggestion fell on *deaf* ears

these words are so embedded in our
language that it takes active practice
and a conscious effort to break away
from using them, Emily Ladau says

frozen by fear
she was *leaning on* the excuse
I was *oblivious* to the way I hurt her
they *didn't acknowledge* his suggestion

language is constantly evolving, Amy says,
none of us use the perfect word all the time

but effort is everything / it shows that
the dignity of others matters to us

prayerful perpetrators

"God told me to pray for you,"
the stranger tells Amy Kenny
"God wants to heal you!"

prayerful perpetrator

"they always approach me with the
same paternalistic confidence, eager
to rid me of my wheelchair or cane."

prayerful perpetrator

"they are too hyped up on their
divine intervention to realize they
are not the savior of my story."

prayerful perpetrator

"I wish prayerful perpetrators were free
from the lie that I am worth less simply
because my body works differently."

absolutely now

privilege is not having to know
not having to think about it, being

able to ignore it and pretend it's not
there because it doesn't affect you

racism / homophobia / ableism

that last one had barely made it on
my radar / for all my talk of justice

and equity and fairness, there's nothing
about disabled people in my last book

I looked right past it / that changes now

if this was you too, it's not too late
our disabled friends are so gracious

to let us catch up and make up for lost
time / but let's not mistake patience for

get-out-of-urgency-free cards / disability
injustice is taking lives and the time to

end ableism is RIGHT NOW

when did we see you?

if Jesus were talking to the church
that fought against the ADA
in Matthew 25:41-43:

"Depart from me,
for I was in a wheelchair
and you gave me no ramp;
I was d/Deaf,
and you gave me no interpreter;
I was blind,
and you gave me no visual descriptions.
I needed an accessible bathroom,
and you did not install one
because it was too expensive.
I asked you not to insult me by saying 'lame'
and you laughed at me.
I wanted to be included,
and you said it would violate
your faith commitments.
I was disabled,
and you did not accommodate me."

—Amy Kenny

flourish

loving my neighbor
as myself
doesn't mean making
anyone

straight like me
cis like me
white like me
non-disabled like me

it means making the world
a safe, accessible place
for each to be themselves
and flourish as they are

to flourish in Black skin
systemic racism
needs to be dismantled

to flourish as a queer person
we need laws that give queer
and cis/het folks the same rights

to flourish as a disabled person
we need laws that protect
and spaces that accommodate

and so much more but we'll start here

sex and "purity"

WSEX 100.0 FM

if I didn't know better
I might think that the
main point of
christianity is

sex

it's really all
some christians
seem to

talk about
care about
shout about
freak out about
point fingers about
make laws about

s
e
x

SEX

their radio only picks up
that one frequency

same song on repeat

don't have sex except
this kind of sex

and here's what we'll do to you if you
get pregnant because of the sex

and don't say gay
and trans kids can't play

and what's in your pants
and were you born that way?

and transgender people want to
flash your kids in public restrooms

forget about AR-15s in schools
it's drag shows that are dangerous

and gay folks want to turn every
kid gay gay gay and more gay

and it was your fault you got raped
your skirt is too short

and your boobs look too good
what did you expect would happen?

god this song is getting old

sexual abuse

is running rampant in the church
and why wouldn't it be? / the

conditions are perfect / you
unquestioningly submit to male

authority and don't trust yourself
because you're evil and no one

would believe you anyway because
you're powerless / I hope we're

seeing a change in the tides where
victims are finally being believed

and more feel brave enough to
come forward / long-time abusers

are getting exposed / now let's
burn it all down, all the way down

it's just sex

I know purity culture messed me
up, she said, *but I can't get past*

how when you have sex you
give a part of yourself away

but do you really? I said
what makes us think that?

putting a thing in a thing
maybe it's not such a big deal

of course this is pure speculation
on my part as I've never had

casual sex or dating sex
or any kind of sex

besides the married variety

purity rings and other bunk

my biggest fears for my kids
used to be that they'd have sex

before they were married and
walk away from christianity

now my biggest fears for my kids
are that they won't have sex until

they're married and that they'll
want to go back to christianity

ancient purity culture

why doesn't the bible address
premarital sex? / maybe because

girls were property, sold off to
men when puberty hit / getting

maritally raped before they even
knew what premarital sex was

just a receptacle

you do know that people in bible
times thought that the whole damn

baby was in the man's seed and the
woman was just a container for it

to grow in, right? / they used the word
"barren" (inhospitable to life) for

women who couldn't get pregnant /
thought women were just a field to

plant babies in / every time I think
about men realizing for the first time

that the entire microscopic future kid
wasn't in their seed / and their spawn

were actually half their mom, I laugh

retch

as a new bride I did something
for my husband in bed that he

asked me to do that literally
made me gag and almost vomit

every single time until
I finally said no more

I also swallowed whatever
evangelical christianity told me

even if it made me gag
which it often did until

I finally said no more
to that too

from blushing bride to wedded wife

grudgingly spent $20 on used copies
of four books I wrote over a decade

ago so I could remember what I used
to think/feel/believe back in the day

took me a minute (months) to open
the first one, a self-help book for

young wives / some of it is cute,
funny, but my stomach lurched

when I read my smug and haughty
purity-culture-fraught admonitions

my question is: how was I so beaten
down *and* so arrogant all at once?

dear complementarian wives

I see you over there loudly proudly
upholding the patriarchy and feel ill

sadly I recognize my younger self in you

some of you were born to lead and speak
and since that's forbidden under the

prescribed gender roles you adhere to,
you cheer on the misogynistic hierarchy

y'all are just as toxic as your men

not my problem

Jesus didn't
tell women
to cover up
their bodies
he told men
to gouge out
their eyes

sick of men

Jesus cast seven demons out of Mary Magdalene
(so they say) / womanist theologian Renita J. Weems

says ancient people believed in good spiritual beings
(angels) and bad (demons) / people with mental

disorders were "possessed" by evil spirits / Mary M
was said to have "demons" because she was a gifted

and charismatic woman in a repressive and
patriarchal society and Jesus gave her freedom to

lead and bloom / sounds familiar / women under
the thumb of complementarianism and patriarchy

prevented from *reaching for, stretching toward,
and developing into* the women god created us to be

Weems writes of women *trying to juggle the
inordinate demands of families and jobs* and I feel

that / my ex was more than happy to let me shoulder
all the weight, adding extra burdens for fun

and for Black women and other women of color,
white supremacy adds a few more layers

spiritual warfare

the night before I'd speak to
christian women's groups about

sex and marriage and motherhood
my husband and I would often get

into a big fight and he could be so
unreasonable and illogical / *it has*

to be satan attacking my marriage,
I'd think, *because it's too absurd not*

to be but I eventually realized that
he was just that irrational on his own

or maybe it was mama god trying to
save those poor women from my

persuasive powers of toxic
complementarian indoctrination

I guess we'll never know

patriarchy

penis promise

why would we get instructions
about gender from an ancient text

written in a time and place when
women were property, holes for

penises, wombs for children, barely
considered human, good for nothing

more than taking care of kids and
dicks for life? / they didn't even

matter enough to be included in
God's phallocentric covenant with

"his" people / don't worry I'm not
sad to be excluded / please keep your

knife away from my skin thanks

scaredy-ass dudes

is it just me or is the bible filled
with stories of brave women and

cowardly men? / this ancient book
often praises women for doing

"men" things better than men / you'd
think the text with its hints of things

like equality and justice and love
sprouting from a toxic patriarchal

culture could show us how to fight
for women's rights but no let's use

it to subjugate women instead / the
bible often uplifted women counter-

culturally and progressively yet
21st century men see it as license

to oppress / what is this fuckery?

exposed

don't tell me that men in a patriarchal
system care about protecting women

nope, they only protect themselves
pastors protect themselves / police

protect themselves / politicians protect
themselves / men aren't protecting us

they're taking us and our bodies into
their own hands, offices, and laws

women don't need protection, Meghan
Tschanz says, *if men stop hurting them*

suffocating

the only ones who can breathe
in this toxic religion are the

white cishet men with their
feet on everybody else's neck

it's mama god for me

"I think it's ridiculous to think of God as
anything that could possibly be gendered.

But as long as the expression of God
as female is unimaginable to many

while the expression of God as male
feels perfectly acceptable—

and as long as women continue to be
undervalued and abused and

controlled here on Earth—
I'll keep using it."

—Glennon Doyle

the sacred Black feminine

"She is the God who is with
and for Black women because

She is a Black woman.

She is the God who definitively declares
that Black women—who exist below Black
men and white women at the bottom of the
white male God's social pecking order—not
only matter but are sacred.

And, in doing so, She declares that
all living beings are sacred.

She is the God who smashes the
white patriarchy and empowers us all
to join in Her liberating work."

—Christena Cleveland

spice it up

all theology has an adjective, Pete Enns
says / what I thought of as "theology"

was really *white patriarchal supremacy
theology* / every theology book I read

was by a white author and affirmed my
already-established views about the

inerrant, infallible, divinely-inspired god-
breathed bible / you know, *solid* theology

the kind without a descriptor / not like:

*womanist theology
Mujerista theology
Black liberation theology
queer theology
red lip theology*

which are the only kinds of theology
I'm interested in these days

she-god

ruach, the word for *spirit*
in Genesis 1:2
(and so many other verses)
is feminine

"The gendering of God's Spirit
as feminine calls for the
feminine pronoun, yet
generations of sexist translations
have gotten around this by
religiously avoiding the pronoun altogether...

feminists and womanists
advocating for inclusive and
explicitly feminine God-language
are not changing but restoring the text
and could be considered biblical literalists."

—Wilda Gafney

p.s. if you're a seminary grad who has
never read *Womanist Midrash*, there's
a hole in your theological training

from subservient to subversive

when submitting to male
authority was no longer

tenable, Sue Monk Kidd
turned to other women

who were *voicing truths*
that had once been unsayable

and that is exactly the kind
of woman I want to be

"christian" nation

you sit on a throne of lies

the story white people tell ourselves
the story "patriotic" Americans tell themselves
the story billionaires tell the rest of us
the story colonizers tell the colonized
the story the 45th president tells his fans
the story Fox news tells its viewers
the story the GOP tells their constituents
the story my ex-husband tells himself
the story mall santa tells the kids on his lap
the story conservative christians tell the world

none of them are true

pernicious

"white christian nationalism" is a phrase 50%
of people don't know, Dr. Jemar Tisby says

the people who adhere to this ideology
just know it as *christianity*

and that's what's so harmful and insidious
and pernicious about it, he says

so many people don't recognize it for what it is

it is so ubiquitous, so common, so normal
in their lives that it just seems like plain old

christianity

you're welcome

just when you think
your rage has settled,

you read
Christians Against Christianity

go buy and read this book
immediately

do not pass go
do not collect $200

this twisted strand of christianity

"That's how I would characterize
Christianity in America today.
A travesty, a brutal sham,
a tragic charade, a cynical deceit.

Why? Because the loudest voices
in American Christianity today—
those of right-wing evangelicals—
shamelessly spew a putrid stew
of religious ignorance and
political venom that is
poisoning our society,
making a mockery of the
Gospel of Jesus Christ.

Their rhetoric in the name
of their Lord and Savior
is mean-spirited, divisive,
appallingly devoid of love
for their neighbors
and outright demonizes
those who do not accept
their narrow views—
even fellow Christians."

—Obery M. Hendricks Jr.

the onus is on us

Marla, please stop saying
christians *when you mean*

republicans *because you are*
making good christians look bad

well, for starters, 81% of evangelical
christians voted for trump

and also I'm not here to protect the
reputation of the "good" christians

I'm here to stop the harm being
done by christians at large

not all christians / prove it
not all republicans / prove it

not all men / prove it
not all white people / prove it

and use actions,
not words

true colors

want to know who's hurting? / who
could use a loving hand? / just look

at who the christians are picking on
this week—more precisely, being

cruel and hateful to / lashing out at
anyone brave enough to question,

uncover lies, speak truth / instead of
defending their position they spout

hateful threats / you'll know we're
christians by our what was that again?

mouths of babes

when I'd ask my 3-year-old
which shirt she wanted to wear,
she'd get her phrases mixed up

I don't matter
or
it doesn't care

what do a lot of people think
of when they hear the words
"evangelical christianity"?

I don't matter
or
it doesn't care

rated R for violence

white supremacy is violent
the patriarchy is violent

substitutionary atonement is violent
eternal hellfire is violent

the god of the OT is violent
christian enslavers were violent

manifest destiny was violent
guns are violent

so much v-i-o-l-e-n-c-e
no thank you

when in Rome

Paul's Roman citizenship came with
privileges he wanted to keep so he told

the enslaved to obey their masters, said
government is ordained of god / guess

who wasn't a Roman citizen? / Jesus /
folks who love Paul more than Jesus

are telling on themselves / they too
have privilege they want to keep / like

perhaps the white kind / we white folks
want to identify with Jesus but Howard

Thurman says his social position in
Palestine was more like that of

Black people in the U.S. of A.

white
supremacy

get your people

when Black friends tell me to get *my people*
that would be white evangelical christians

those are my people, where I come from, and
it's why I'm not swearing them off for good

once we wake up it's our duty and obligation
to reach those in our inner circles with the truth

some disowned me but I can gather the rest
anyone who shows the smallest desire to learn

and grow and do better / those who refuse to
wake from sleep will waste our time and suck

our energy / MLK sat in Birmingham Jail 60
years ago, said white christians were going too

slow / what have we fucking done since then?

so sick of this

"It is hardly a moral act to
encourage others patiently
to accept injustice which
he himself does not endure."

—Martin Luther King Jr.

synonymous / ominous

nationalism, homophobia, xenophobia,
white supremacy have become so conflated

with being a christian that a fight against
one of those evils is perceived as an assault

on christianity / imagine thinking that
fighting racism = attacking christianity

and yet here we are

do the math

how can we claim to care
about Black lives but vote

for the dude that 91% of
Black voters voted against?

the numbers don't lie / they
tell a story / are we listening?

king jaded himself

"I love the pure, peaceable, and
impartial Christianity of Christ;

I therefore hate the corrupt,
slaveholding, women-whipping,
cradle-plundering, partial, and
hypocritical Christianity of this land.

Indeed, I can see no reason,
but the most deceitful one, for calling
the religion of this land Christianity.

I look upon it as the climax
of all misnomers,
the boldest of all frauds,
and the grossest of all libels."

—Frederick Douglass

whom shall I answer?

the enslaver sits down to a meal
prepared for him by people he owns

thank you god for every good
thing you've blessed me with
multiply the fruits of my labor

the enslaved woman—exhausted,
bruised, pregnant with his child prays

please god deliver me and my children
from the abuse of this evil man
we can't bear this much longer

are they praying to the same god?
or does the color of god's skin

change according to the petitioner?
who does god love more?

I will never understand a god who
sends plagues on the Egyptians and

drowns their army so enslaved
Israelites can go free but lets white

Americans brutalize and enslave
their fellow humans with impunity

scripture as chains

Howard Thurman's grandmother, who took
care of him for much of his childhood, was

born into slavery / one of his chores was
to read to her because she had never

learned how / he would read Psalms, the
gospels, parts of Isaiah, but never ever

any of Paul's epistles / she wouldn't let
him / when he was older he asked her why /

she said that her master's white minister
held occasional services for the enslaved

people on the plantation and his text was
always from Paul, most often *slaves be*

obedient to your masters and "I promised
my Maker," she said, "that if I ever learned

to read and if freedom ever came, I
would not read that part of the Bible"

and she kept her word

preach, sister

the great evangelist D. L. Moody who
died in 1899 and is lauded to this day

by christians who name buildings and
institutions and radio stations after him

segregated his revivals to appease racist
white southerners / and Black activist

Ida B. Wells had something to say about it

Our American Christians are too busy
saving the souls of white Christians

from burning in hellfire to save the lives
of black ones from present burning

in fires kindled by white Christians.

amen amen amen / and how many of
these christians were going to revivals

then coming home and lynching Black
people? / a whole bunch of them

"defending" god

you refused to be
in a photo with me

because my shirt said
Black Lives Matter

we had a long talk and
I tried to convince you

that no, BLM doesn't
hate god, and no, they

aren't out to destroy
anyone's *traditional family*

in all fairness, I wouldn't
be in a photo with you

if you had a MAGA hat on
but just so you know

that's apples and oranges
my shirt simply states that

Black Lives Matter and
that red hat is code for

no they don't

blanca theologia sola

put down this book
check your shelves
do you see...

Lisa Sharon Harper / Wilda Gafney
James H. Cone / Drew G. I. Hart
Osheta Moore / Candice Benbow
Christena Cleveland / Renita J. Weems
Jacqui Lewis / Jemar Tisby
Trey Ferguson / Robert Monson
Howard Thurman / Willie James Jennings
Katie Cannon / Danté Stewart
Mitzi J. Smith / Kelly Brown Douglas
Claude Atcho / Cole Arthur Riley

I read Black theologians so I can
understand why someone would

still want to be a christian after all
that oppression / and because we

can't understand the full breadth and
depth of the bible if we only read it

through the eyes of white people

we would never say *white is right*
but our reading habits say it for us

refined palate

"Because of the gospel
that was fed
to my ancestors
against their will,
I inspect
my Good News
closely
before consuming it."

—Trey Ferguson

not your business

a "concerned" white man
once said to Black theologian

Katie Cannon: *well it seems*
to me that womanist work

is not talking about white
people and Katie replied:

that is correct / we do not
begin or end our work with

white people on our eyeballs

well it seems to me that
learning about womanism

and celebrating it means
supporting something that

isn't *for* me and doesn't
include me and it is far

past time for us white folks
to decenter ourselves

we wrestle with it

"No matter how misogynistic,
how heavily redacted,

how death-dealing, how troubled,
troubling, or troublesome the text,

womanists who teach and preach
in the black church do not throw

the whole androcentric text with its
patriarchal and kyriarchal lowlights

out of our stained-glass windows
because of its Iron Age theology.

We wrestle with it because
it has been received as Scripture."

—Wilda Gafney

not my place

christianity isn't mine to throw out
enslaved Africans in the U.S. made

something beautiful and hopeful out
of it, made it their own, somehow saw

through the brutal hell of chattel slavery
and recognized something they could

cling to in hope / I can only speak to the
corrupted white evangelical version

dirty or clean?

"Healing involves discomfort—
but so does refusing to heal…

Clean pain is pain that mends
and can build your capacity for growth…

Dirty pain is the pain of
avoidance, blame, and denial…

A key factor in the perpetuation
of white-body supremacy
is many people's refusal
to experience clean pain
around the myth of race.

Instead, usually out of fear,
they choose the dirty pain of
silence and avoidance and,
invariably, prolong the pain."

—Resmaa Menakem

god loveth a cheerful giver

thank you, evangelical christianity
for conditioning me to give 10% of

my income to the church without
blinking even when I could barely

pay my bills / now I happily pay micro-
reparations so my Black siblings can

find joy and rest / I highly recommend
this purer form of tithes and offerings

his ancestors' wildest dreams

"I used to think talking
about Black life,
or even Black faith,
was about convincing
white people to be better.

But that's far too limiting.

No—I've learned that
talking about Blackness
is about giving us words;
setting our bodies free;
living in ways that we feel
seen, inspired, protected…

Life is not just fight—
it is also love."

—Danté Stewart

colonization

rice christians

revivals in Africa! she claimed
432 salvations! praise god!

oh that's wonderful and I'm
sure it has nothing to do with

the free chickens you handed
out at the end? / if my kids were

hungry I'd repeat some white
lady's words for a meal too

what would be great is if you
offered to help me feed my kids

or earn a sustainable income with
no salvation-strings attached

pet peeve

christians who have
EVERYTHING + Jesus

telling people who have
NOTHING

that all they need is
JESUS

vanity trip

off we jet in our little homogenous group
with matching t-shirts, suitcases full of

toys / excited about our carefully curated
experience that our hosts know will give

us stories to tell but won't rock our world
too big / missions trips aren't as helpful

as we wish they were / they're for the
benefit of the go-er, not the hosts and it's

dishonest to say otherwise / they know your
plane ticket cost $2000, the food you gave

them cost $2 / they've built their own houses /
held their own babies / done their own

laundry / for generations / *but getting your
hands dirty teaches you so much!* / think

about why you'll spend $3000 on a trip
but not give $3000 and stay home / I'm

not saying the trip didn't change your life
but stop pretending it saved theirs

bum sprayers or bust

in the U.S. we train kids to go in diapers
only to have to untrain them in two years

we adults train our bodies to release our
bowels in an unnatural position—seated

on a toilet instead of squatting / when
our bowels won't move we buy stools

to bring our feet up level with our bodies
wipe poop with dry toilet paper, then

spend hundreds of dollars trying to make
it soft enough not to chafe and burn when

a simple rinse would do the trick / you
don't realize these things until you live

in a country with better ways of doing
things and now I get a little pissy when

American christians arrogantly assume
that we're the smart "developed" ones

the mythical melting pot

many North American christians want
reassurance that the white dominant

culture will remain undisturbed and will
continue to be the norm, Karen González says

assimilation makes her uncomfortable
because it requires her to *celebrate the loss*

of other people's culture, traditions, and
languages in order to alleviate the fears that

white people, including Christians, might
have about a diverse society where their

position as power broker might be threatened
she's not about to absolve anyone of their

responsibility to welcome and love immigrants
it is not my job to appease privileged white

Christians at the expense of the dignity
of immigrants / amen to that

poisoned blankets

we claim to be bringing
god to people

who desperately
need a savior

but really we're
just bringing

white supremacy
and toxicity

disease and destruction
and death

it's a centuries-long
pattern with us

a church called Freedom

fired from a ministry in Cambodia for
"losing confidence in our director" and

our pastor swooped in like a vulture on
a fresh kill / said he couldn't have been

happier because god gave him a
dream about "our family walking the

neighborhood inviting people to church"
how do you argue with a pastor whose

"divine dream" looks and sounds exactly
like what your heart longs for—loving

your neighbors / how did that story end? /
oh we "lost confidence in our pastor" / he

hated it when those under his authority
questioned his motives and actions / like

a wise friend said, "*Jesus* isn't the king
of Freedom Church / the *pastor* is"

144

co-lo-ni-zing

white missionaries and pastors tell
young impressionable brown christians

in Cambodia to divest from their "evil"
culture to follow Jesus / *if your brother's*

wedding is on a Sunday, skip it and go
to church instead / show god he's more

important than your family / a young
friend's parents gave her a garment as

protection from evil spirits but she
wanted to trust Jesus to protect her and

asked for my advice / I gently suggested
it was okay to honor her parents / if a

tradition is harmful, that's one thing but
you don't have to forsake your culture

because a white person at church
said you're disappointing Jesus

reverse missionary

it took me five years of
living in a southeast Asian

country to realize how white
and western we've made god

I used to tell people they were
sinners and needed Jesus

now I tell Jesus-followers
they're sinning against people

and need to make reparations
I want Black and Indigenous

people to reclaim what white
christians stole—their land,

labor, bodies, rituals, dances
the list is forever long

we have to give it back
give it back give it back

holy pot meet kettle

my Somali friends wouldn't call
their babies beautiful because

evil spirits might take notice and
try to harm them / silly, right?

yet no different from me trying to
convince god I loved him more

than I loved my kids so he
wouldn't take them from me

the irony and audacity of me
thinking that people in other

religions worshiped their gods
out of fear when I worshiped

mine out of love / yeah right

that would have been nice

my kid wishes we could have
just been "normal" neighbors

to our muslim friends instead
of looking at everybody as

potential converts and loving
them with ulterior motives

*why couldn't we have just
chilled?* she wants to know

I wish I had an answer

the pain of decolonization

it's not just an overseas phenomenon
I have so many Black and brown friends

on this continent too who got caught up
in white evangelical christianity that

told them to forsake their families and
culture / whiteness is always demanding

assimilation and it's never more blatantly
obvious than in the white evangelical

church / of course you don't ever mention
whiteness / you hide behind Jesus and

denying yourself and making kingdom
sacrifices / it's all a bunch of bullshit, and

when my Black and brown siblings wake
up to the lies and the evil toxicity it can be

hard to go back home because they often
left their families and culture to worship

white Jesus / it hurts my heart to see
them try to heal a pain I'll never know

make it make at least a little bit of sense

when we lived in Cambodia, my 16-year-old
tutor and I would take turns reading through

the new testament in our second languages
a Khmer lesson for me and English practice

for her / when we got to first Corinthians
seven, she asked, "what is *circumcised*?"

my Khmer bible just said *cut skin* because
the practice and the word are non-existent

in Cambodia / *cut skin* could mean anything
and I didn't know the Khmer word for *penis*

so I called my daughter in for back-up to
help me explain this holy male-only custom

so much for the bible being clear and taking
it literally across all cultures I guess

modern western-colored glasses

we know-it-all American christians
have the hardest time understanding

the bible because our culture is so
far removed from theirs / my Khmer

friends have no trouble picturing a
mama hen gathering her chicks under

her wings like god does or the true
nativity scene, a home where extended

family cohabits, someone has a baby
and cows live in the house / they can

also appreciate foot washing as a
true act of love because everyone

walks dirt roads in sandals / and
taking clean socks off doesn't quite

pack the same punch / bottom line?
we don't have a clue

sit with this

I'm suspicious of anyone who can
observe colonization, genocide, and

decay in the world and not be stirred
to lament in some way, Cole Arthur

Riley writes / me too / her ancestors
were *abducted from their homes, raped,*

and enslaved / and she *will not be rushed*
out of [her] sorrow for it / if we're not

lamenting, then we're probably in denial
and there will never ever be any kind of

whole and healthy world until
there's a big ol' reckoning

where privilege comes from

my friend Rohadi gets asked on the
regular—*where are you from?* so

people can determine whether or not
he belongs here (wherever *here* is)

if you're white, Rohadi says, *you get
a free, no-questions-asked pass to*

*belong in virtually every public space
and that,* he says, *is an inheritance*

*rooted in the spoils of
colonization and domination*

vibranium

"Buried in the heart of every Black person
is a sliver of vibranium.

How could anything else possibly be true?

…Vibranium feels like the metaphorical distillation
of what makes us us.

What else could represent the ways that
Black people have turned pain into power
and used it for a collective good?

The Black American experience has been about
the unfathomable and beautiful ways we've
absorbed, stored, and released the various energies

that have assaulted and surrounded us
since being forcibly brought
to the North American shores centuries ago.

For us, vibranium is putting a name
to the thing we've used to develop
our identity, our culture, and our future.

…I'm here to tell you that vibranium is real."

—Tre Johnson

a breather

almost too much

trauma you've seen
trauma you've felt
trauma you've caused

it's a lot

then add a pandemic
and all the upheaval
and anxiety and fear

it's a lot

I just want to
acknowledge that
and give us space

to sit
to breathe
to feel

cause it's a
whole whole lot

take a deep breath

inhale, exhale
it's okay

you don't have to unlearn
every toxic thing *today*

you don't have to undo
all of white supremacy *today*

you don't have to help
all of everybody *today*

go outside and run your
fingers through the grass

or sit on the couch
and look out the window

close your eyes
take a rest

know that you are loved
not for what you do

but because you're *you*
and you're not alone

we're in this together

whatever you feel right now

acknowledge it
feel it
embrace it
honor it

and turn the page
whenever you're ready

mama earth

heaven help us all

I used to think
any mention of
mother earth
was a slap
in the face
of the one true
father god

forgive me

in my past life,
I thought
why waste time
saving the planet?

we need to save souls

now I know that
we lost our souls

when we
colonized
exploited
dominated
raped
capitalized on
mama earth

save her and
we might just

get our souls back

creation stories matter

because they *tell us who we are*
Robin Wall Kimmerer says

even if we're not thinking of them,
we're *inevitably shaped by them*

Skywoman *created a garden*
for the well-being of all

Eve was banished from a garden
for tasting fruit from a tree
forced to earn her food
by the sweat of her brow

to eat she had to *subdue the*
wilderness into which she was cast

same species / same earth
different stories

one woman is our *ancestral gardener*
leading us to *a generous embrace*
of the living world

the other was an exile, just passing
through an alien world on a rough road
to her real home in heaven

162

ode to my tree family

I didn't know much
about your healing powers
until these past two years

a global pandemic
betrayal and divorce
repatriation in a new place

a breast cancer scare
worries about my kids
etc etc etc

and there you were
tall and strong

such pretty green
against the blue sky

such a sweet home
for birds and squirrels

kindly sharing space with me
so constant so faithful so true

I found god in you
and I found myself
in you too

thoughts on land acknowledgments

when is something better than nothing
and when is a gesture just not enough?

this book was written on the
traditional and unceded lands of the

Tsalaguwetiyi and Congaree peoples who
in spite of every effort to destroy them—

European colonization, displacement,
land theft, residential schools, genocide—

are still here

we owe them so much more than a simple
acknowledgment, the smallest of first steps

toward learning the truth of history, making
things right, honoring Indigenous peoples,

mother earth, and all our relations, opening
our purses to give back what we stole

back deck church

the trees greet and welcome
the pine cones open in prayer

the bees recite scripture
the dragonfly entertains the wee ones

one bird sings a lament
another a song of praise

the hawk preaches a sermon
the leaves say amen

the squirrels collect the offering
the crow gives the benediction

I sit in wonder, taking it all in
no one pressures me in any way
I am free to just be

all are welcome
all belong
all together

I'm home

thanksgiving address

the Haudenosaunee begin every
gathering by greeting and thanking
each living thing that sustains us

school children on reservations start
each morning not with a pledge to a
flag but a thank you to all living things

thank you, Mother Earth
thank you, deep blue waters
thank you, tall green grasses

thank you, sweet fruits and berries
thank you, fish in the rivers
thank you, corn, beans, and squash

thank you, forest animals
thank you, beautiful trees
thank you, singing birds

thank you, Grandfather Beings
thank you, Elder Brother Sun
thank you, Grandmother Moon

what a beautiful way to live

queerly beloved

n-o-p-e

I treat queer people with
value and dignity, she says
I just can't affirm their lifestyle

hold up

if the person I'm "valuing" and
"dignifying" doesn't *feel* valued
or dignified, it doesn't count

love doesn't feel like hate

love
does
not
feel
like
hate

LOVE DOES NOT FEEL LIKE HATE

please
stop
saying
it
does

it's really not that hard

you really can't keep track
of everyone's pronouns, huh?

I bet you can

I know 8 Richards
and have no problem
remembering
which ones go by

Rick
Rich
Richard
Dick

hell, I'd call them Muffy
if they asked me to

think of it as an opportunity
to be reasonable and
considerate of others

the alternative is to double
down in stubbornness

it's our choice

we can easily afford this

what does it cost us to honor another
person's experience or identity? trans

theologian Shannon Kearns asks / *what*
does it cost us to use the name and

pronouns that are correct? / not much
he says / a little discomfort, some possible

embarrassment, a learning curve / on
the flip side, *the cost is deadly, but*

cisgender people are not the ones to pay it
the burden is on those who are already

oppressed and marginalized; the cost is
paid by the very people who cannot

afford to pay it / the words we use to
describe people should come from *them*

what does it cost us to ask someone their
preferred pronouns and then use them?

so very little / get your wallet out

amen and then some

"Being queer is magical.
It ruins every blueprint
the empire has
for their polite society
and shows how expansive
and creative human potential is.
Queerness is the leading edge
of God's creation."

—Kevin Garcia

dealbreaker

my friend is LGBTQ+ affirming
but her church isn't, says
anyone who meets me there
will know I'm a safe space

if you're a safe space,
but your church isn't,
you're still inviting them
into an unsafe place

I'm not inviting people, but
anyone who comes will find me
welcoming, not judging
I can't control other church folks

if my kid/friend/neighbor is gay
and my church says being gay is a sin
and my person can't be a full part,
then why would I keep going there?

sorry my church
doesn't welcome you
but I choose my church

not me / I choose my loved ones

take a stand

"I hate it
when Christians
love queer actors,
queer shows,
queer singers,
but in real life
they're not affirming.
It's not fair."

—my kid

it all evens out in the end

you're sending people to hell if
you let them stay gay, Marla

oh, the evangelism point system?

for every person I lead in the
salvation prayer, I get a point?

for every person I send to hell by
letting them stay gay, I lose two?

any idea how many folks I've
"saved?" / most of them kids (gah!)

it'll be a minute before you pass
me on the conversion leaderboard

if I let my gay friends stay gay and
you don't *have* any gay friends

then we've both sent aaallll the gay
folks to hell collectively / go team!

p.s. if you need me I'll be
in hell with my queer friends

get your Greek on

if you believe it's wrong to be gay
because "the bible says so" and

you've never taken time to read
about the culture and languages

those words were written in or
learned that the word "homosexual"

wasn't in the bible until 1946 or
that the bible explicitly says

Sodom's sin was not feeding the
poor, then your beliefs are lazy and

harmful / if you do the studying and
exegeting with a posture of learning,

then conclude it's a sin, okay—you're
not lazy but your beliefs still cause

harm / it took me too long to see the
truth / it's straight cis privilege to take

our sweet cis time deciding if queer
people are on a highway to hell

meant to be

is there anything
more beautiful
than when
trans people
get to finally be
on the outside
who they've
always been
on the inside?

as seen on

this is the gay
that the lord
has made

let us rejoice
and be glad
with them

—a bumper sticker

177

you know what I love?

seeing queer christians showing love to
non-affirming christians and winning

'em to the Jesus way of truly loving
everyone and I can't stop grinning over

it / and yes I realize this calling is not
for everyone / god knows I'm not that

good / it takes a special kind of person
to be so gracious and patient and

undeservedly kind / may god pour
blessings over their sweet queer heads

pro-"life"

a god who cares about babies

When Herod realized that he had been
outwitted by the Magi, he was furious,
and he gave orders to kill all the boys
in Bethlehem and its vicinity who were
two years old and under, in accordance
with the time he had learned from the Magi.

—Matthew 2:16

"The baby Jesus escapes Herod's attempt
to murder the King of the Jews, but many
babies do not. Many mothers who could not
cross the border into Egypt because of poverty
or detainment watched their children being
slaughtered. Is the reader invited to stop and
mourn them? Could not God protect God's
Messiah son *and* the other children as well?"

—Mitzi J. Smith

A voice is heard in Ramah,
weeping and great mourning,
Rachel weeping for her children
and refusing to be comforted,
because they are no more.

—Matthew 2:18

180

when you put it that way

atheist Sam Harris's thoughts on 20%
of pregnancies ending in miscarriage:

*if God exists, He is the most
prolific abortionist of all*

under the influence

a few short years ago I would have been
gleeful over the overturn of Roe v. Wade

today I'm sad, sick, scared / I know I
can't persuade anyone that it's a really

bad and harmful decision / because I
was *that person* for 40+ years and

becoming pro-choice took me a decade
of deconstruction to arrive at / so much

else came first / nobody goes from
vehemently pro-life to adamantly

pro-choice after reading a Facebook
post or handful of poems / I know every

single bit of the argument by heart and
when that was me, there wasn't a damn

thing a single damn person could say to
dissuade me from my truth

bedmates

pro-"life" was everything to me, the
granddaddy of them all / so deeply

indoctrinated into me / the end of my
slippery slope, the final piece of my

deconstruction puzzle, the very last
domino to fall / what toppled it? / the

blatant disregard for human life at
every damn turn / every other thing

evangelical christians fought for or
against in the "culture wars" turned out

to be code for other things entirely,
things that caused great harm to people

and also? / just happened to coincide with
their insatiable lust for power and control

checkmate

the religious right recruited us
to fight for them / called us

soldiers for christ / turns out we
were fighting for white male

christian dominance / lowly pawns
in their toxic/shitty game of chess

I did a little digging

into evangelicals' absolutely
laser-focused, single-issue
obsession with abortion

was it born out of a deep
sense of love and care for
precious womb-dwellers?

of course not / it was a sham
a crock, a cover-up for racism

the great "family values"
man James Dobson himself
is on record in 1973 saying

he didn't believe a fetus
was a human being

it wasn't until 1979 that
evangelicals faked outrage
over abortion as cover

for their real campaign:
protecting segregated schools

it was the perfect political scam
and we all completely fell for it

something's off

I care about
the unborn
and women

she told me

and the poor
and the rich
and immigrants
and Black people
and queer people
and and and

I believe you, I said

but out of that whole list
the GOP only "cares" about

unborn babies
(okay and the rich)

and isn't that just
a little bit suspicious?

how I see it

love them both
as evangelical
catchphrase
is a chimera

you can't fight for
unborn babies
AND
women

but fight for
women
and you'll save
all kinds of lives

you lied to me

hey pro-life politician
when given the opportunity
to truly care for life, to prevent
abortions even, you said
no, no, no, never, no
no support for single moms
no free birth control
no safety net
no affordable healthcare
no gun laws to protect kids in schools
no mercy for immigrants
no no no no no
you don't care about life
you want to control people
you exploit the unborn
for your political agenda
you picked the most vulnerable,
helpless, the only literally
voiceless group there is
so you can win seats and
elections and money and power
I voted for you three times
and never ever again

guns > kids

evangelicals used to frame school
shootings as an opportunity for

martyrdom but that got harder and
harder to do the more shootings there

were and the younger the victims got
six-year-olds are kind of tiny to be

laying down their lives for christians'
individual rights, freedom, and power

morbidity

you say pro-life while
immersed in a culture of death

selling enslaved women's
children / ripping Indigenous

children from their homes
separating families at the border

fixated on the crucifixion
obsessed with guns

supposedly picking up your
cross and dying to self

any "help" you give isn't
promised until after death

withholding aid
turning away refugees

looking the other way
while people suffer and die

me too

"I'm so damn tired of politics
that use people's bodies and
personhood as opportunities
for cultural warfare."

—Rev. Dr. Jacqui Lewis

you can't

force people
to give birth

then refuse
to help them

raise their
babies

watch us,
they said

infidelity

two true things

you were
really
hard to love

and I
really
loved you hard

is this a poem
about my ex
or christianity?

I often think

I can't trust myself
because I didn't know

my husband was cheating
on me for four years

but it was the
patriarchal
misogynistic
christian
brainwashing

that didn't allow me to even
consider the thought

I was tricked into thinking
that morality and fidelity

were as important to him
as they were to me

spoiler: they were not

to my ex

I see now
how you made
all those
judgmental
and hateful
comments
about adulterers
and "sluts"
just to throw me
off your scent
a well-known tactic
used by all kinds of
religious leaders
mired in the same
exact stuff they
self-righteously
condemn in others
and I won't fall
for it again

it's better to know

I thought my marriage was solid
sure my husband could be a little
shitty but he was faithful

and then it crumbled and everything
I knew to be true was a lie

speaking of lies and crumbles
how about when you find out

the truth about U.S. history
the truth about evangelical christianity
the truth about the pro-life movement
the truth about our complicity

it hurts like hell but eventually you're
so grateful to have uncovered the truth

and now it's chin up and time to
help others escape the deception

his "apology" in its entirety

I know some people, maybe you,
are angry or disappointed
with my choices this past year
(leaving my wife, moving halfway
around the world and not seeing
my children for 7 months).
You're allowed to feel that way.

my ex wrote on Facebook in April 2021

Even through my shame I will praise God
for who He is. For every minute of
extended life He had planned to give me.
I am not here today to suck anything else out of life
but to direct you away from myself and toward Him.
Regardless of the hate you have for me,
He deserves your admiration.

dude you forgot the

having sex with another woman
for four years while I was married
and posing as a missionary

part

and my phone lights up

he hides his true self
in a veil of religion

my friend texts me

wearing a cloak of
false righteousness and
a mask of "godliness"

rebuking actual truth
and justifying himself with
a flow of Christianese

it has nothing to do with Jesus
and everything to do with
hypocritical posturing

it's all so gross
and so insincere
and so harmful

I thank her and cry

not my god

every
single
word
you've
said
about
god
while
being
married
to
me
and
fucking
someone
else's
wife
is
dead
to
me

her body knew

a few years ago my very very
sensitive intuitive daughter

developed an aversion to her dad
didn't want him to touch her

he gives me the creeps

it broke my heart / I prayed
my heart out / I cried and cried

over it / spoke in tongues over it
god, heal their relationship but

god was silent / my prayers went
unanswered / years later, after he

left and I found out about his
betrayal, I made the connection

the timing was precise / he started
cheating and she felt it in her bones

don't touch me / you're creepy

damn if only I'd had her intuition
or maybe I had it and ignored it

kings and queens

your mom likens you to king David
on Facebook, a man after god's own

heart / she didn't mean the part about
the adultery and raping a woman less

powerful than you but that's what I
hear / she also claims our marriage

was loveless for years / not true / I
loved you / while you alternated

between pretending to love me and
being awful to me / if I was the one

who cheated on her son for years,
then abandoned him and our kids

to live with my lover across the
world but I talked big words about

god, would she compare me to
David too? or pick other names?

like Jezebel? / or maybe just whore?

same same and not very different

a Cambodian friend says my ex's
incessant posts about god remind

him of people who screw up, hurt
their families and become monks so

people can find a way to like them
again / they've ruined their reputation

this is their only hope / even if they
don't care about religion one little bit

they have to pretend they do

better end of the bargain

we split all our crap
down the middle

half for me
half for you

I got our
beautiful children

and I let you keep
your "god"

curses

I don't pray
a whole lot these
days but after
the stunt you
pulled today
I'm going to
open my bible
halfway down
the middle and
find the most
imprecatory Psalm
I possibly can
and insert your
name into it
and recite it daily
until it comes true

both/and

he's a jerk and you're
better off without him

I appreciate the sentiment
and know you say it in love

but it also minimizes my
pain and sorrow and anguish

I'm better off without
evangelical christianity too

but the long brutal journey
to get to the other side

was full of loss and grief
and heartbreak

stagnant

faith of a child

do you think that means just
rehashing what you learned

at age five, wearing the same
brain grooves over and over

no new neural pathways
ever being formed?

a child is curious,
asks questions,
wants to know *how*
and *why* all day long

now I do too

we can't mistake
stymied growth
for "standing firm"

inertia isn't the flex
we think it is

our long-held beliefs
could use some scrutiny

you keep

reading
thinking
believing
listening to

the same things

over and
over and
over and
over again

no wonder your brain
muscles are so tight

you've never stretched
your thinking

p.s. it's not too late

that meme where

the caterpillar and butterfly
catch up over coffee

caterpillar: *you've changed*
butterfly: *we're supposed to*

gets me every time

forever in progress

I'm constantly

reviewing
revising
reworking
revamping

my words
my ideas
my beliefs
my life

isn't that kind
of the point?

doubting is healthy

there are years
that ask questions
and years that answer,

Zora Neale Hurston wrote

the problem with
evangelical christianity

is that we got this
turned around

we lived our
"have all the answers"
years first and

when the questions arose
we came unglued

stretch marks

I not only stretched my mother
physically before I was born

and during my birth, Alice Walker
wrote, *I was born to stretch her*

spiritually / her words bring me
comfort and I offer them here to my

fellow gen x'ers deconstructing to
the deep dismay of boomer parents

drinking the kool-aid

as a kid I ate mashed potatoes from
a box and canned veggies galore

I refused the carrots, swallowed
peas whole with my kool-aid

did our parents realize all that
processed food was so unhealthy?

mine figured it out and started making
real mashed potatoes, fresh and

frozen veggies / no more kool-aid
with two cups of sugar in every

pitcher / now if I could just get
them to recognize the toxic in their

canned/boxed/packaged *beliefs*

the christian agnostic

"And what a
releasing moment
of freedom it is when,

having been hampered
by being told
we ought to believe
some improbable thesis
because the church teaches it,
or the Bible states it,

we throw it away and
discard it forever
as the nonsense
it has really always been!"

—Leslie D. Weatherhead (1965)

no more take it easy

once upon a time I was playing
restaurant with my adorable nephew

he asked for my order and I said *I*
would like some ice cream / pronto!

sensing my urgency he returned quickly
with a plastic bowl and spoon and said

here's your ice cream
but we're all out of pronto

I get that you can't rush the journey and
all that but when it comes to injustice

no more slow and steady wins the race when
people are suffering and dying / this isn't

child's play / I don't care what you have to
do but FIND SOME FUCKING PRONTO

church

ennui

I dreaded Sunday mornings
as a kid (and Sunday night)

(and Wednesday night too)
listening to the pastor drone

on and on was the single most
agonizing hour of my week

as a teen I reeeally dreaded it
same story as an adult

as a parent of small kids
I dreaded it so bad

heck I dreaded it as a
parent of big kids too

now as someone who hasn't
gone to church in 5+ years

I am loving life

go to church every Sunday and
go to heaven when you die

or skip church every Sunday
and be in heaven every week

complicit

why don't you try to change the
church from the inside, Marla?

because that would require
following all their rules, ones

that are harming people as we
speak / join Team Oppressor while

I'm trying to free people? / nope
not gonna rush into battle in the

enemy uniform / I respect a lot of
christians working hard to wake

the church up to white supremacy,
to engage in lament over racial

injustices past and present, to
become anti-racist / but I see so

little progress, so little hope / and I
know from experience that there's

only so much *inside* a person
can take before she suffocates

I'm good out here thanks

here's your sign

why not go
to church?

because it feels
too much

like crossing the
picket line

this should not be

"Not once did an atheist or liberal
or leftist make me doubt my faith.

Only two things ever did that:
suffering and church folks.

And a lot of that suffering
came from church folks."

—J. S. Park

more from freedom church

so many red flags, she said, *our*
pastor makes me so uncomfortable

I told her she wasn't alone
I could see them too / it's not okay

I went out of town / she sent me a dm

my husband and I
talked to the pastor
please ignore what I said
I was wrong
I'm submitting to God
and the pastor's leadership
you and I can still be friends
but we can never talk
about him negatively again

no thanks,
I don't do fake friends

especially ones
who enable
abusers

how to get away with spiritual abuse

when someone wakes up
and walks away from
your toxicity

just tell those who stayed,
Marla is listening
to the devil

works like a charm

I get it

I get why people in church are lying
to themselves right now / I did the

same thing in my marriage / I told
myself untruths like *it's not that bad*

and *it's definitely going to get better*
you have to contort and justify and

ignore and cover up anything that
threatens to mess up what you have

YOU NEED TO HAVE THIS
THIS IS WHO YOU ARE

it's your belonging / your family /
your home / your everything / you

built a whole life around the church

come hell, high water, or heretic
sisters you must stand firm / you

CANNOT let anything tear it down
CANNOT MUST NOT WILL NOT

collateral damage be damned

guarding my heart

Alice Walker contracted Lyme disease
from ticks without knowing it and it

almost killed her / but she loved the earth
so much and wanted to return to it even

though it hurt her / so "with socks pulled
high and sleeves pulled low" she did

if I ever return to church I'll don a
head-to-toe suit of proverbial armor

as protection / but most likely I'll just
stay out here in the fun and sun in my

comfy t-shirt and shorts and flip-flops
I don't love church enough to risk it

snow thank you

we just got a rare fall of snow
down here in South Carolina

it was fun for the day but
I wasn't sad to see it go

snow / marriage / church

did them for decades, some
good stuff for sure but also

so / much / work

the grief outweighed the joy
it was time for them to go

no thank you

evangelism 101

#1: strip people's rights away
#2: make them suffer endlessly
#3: they'll see they need Jesus
#4: and say that prayer

middle ground

is great for some things like:

I like red and you like blue so
let's compromise with purple

or *I want tacos and you want pizza*
let's order taco pizza

but not so much with

I like racism and
you like not being discriminated
against for being Black

so let's meet in the middle with
half-discrimination or racism lite

or I like abusing my wife and
she likes not being abused
by her husband

so let's meet in the middle and
I'll just abuse you on
Monday Wednesday and Friday

when harm is on the table
we have to choose a side

you need to see both sides

sure if you're a white person
trying to understand Black people

an evangelical christian
trying to understand muslims

a product of public schools
trying to understand unschoolers

but

I'm a liberal agnostic (if we're
labeling) who spent almost four

decades as a zealous conservative
christian / the only side I need to

learn a single other thing about
is the side I'm on right now

and I can't help but notice that the
only people both-sides-ing are the

ones in the wrong much like the
woman who told King Solomon

to go ahead and cut that baby in
two and give half to each of them

advantage: moi

I know your side better
than you know mine

I lived and breathed it for
almost 40 years and as

Obery M. Hendricks Jr.
would say:

I can't be dismissed as
a contentious outsider

crimes against humanity

really tired of christians with planks
of white supremacy and misogyny and

homophobia etc sticking out of their
eyeballs who are so obsessed with itty-

bitty specks of not-even sin in everybody
else's / sin is when you harm other people

period

all for shit

you can't just
love people
without sharing
Jesus,
Marla,
or they'll get
the wrong idea

if you just love
your neighbor
for 20 years
without sharing
the gospel
then what
was the point?

um, love?
love was the point

no you can't pick my brain

God laid you on
my heart

ouch
sounds painful

seriously hon you don't
need to worry about me

a lost cause by your definition
but happy as a clam by mine

allow me to take myself
off your chest

there / that's better

now take a deep breath
and run free

welp

don't got a husband
don't got a pastor
don't got a boss
don't live with my dad

so… who tells you what to do?

I do
I tell me
what to do

but who keeps you in line and
makes up rules for you to follow
and gate-keeps you and such
and whatnot and so on
pray tell?

me, myself, and noooooobody else

can't see a bridge

author Amy Tan says she and her
parents are separated by *a gulf of*

inharmonious beliefs and I feel
this / each time I try to swim to

where they are, the waves are so
rough, I get saltwater up my nose,

in my lungs and start choking, so
lately I've just stayed on the shore

different orchard, Jocelyn

my 90-something relative wrote a
book about the evils of socialism

and it's basically regurgitated Fox
news talking points, half-truths plus

complete untruths and I've never
felt so ill or known an apple to fall

so very very far from a tree

surely not

how do you think you'll
win me back to the lord?

surely not through the exact
same theological arguments

I defended for decades until
I realized they were shit and

surely not by telling me to read
the gospels when I've read all

the way through the bible so
many times already and

surely not by praying
something bad happens

to me so I'll realize
I need Jesus

because a whole lot of bad things
have already happened to me so...

surely not

take me off your prayer list

please I'm asking you nicely / it's
not worth it / I'm not coming back

I'm done swallowing everything I
was spoon-fed / those days are long

gone and anyway why would you try
to pray me back into submission and

subjugation, pray me back into the
smallest meekest version of me?

glory hallelujah amen

I feel like you can't
possibly understand
how happy I am not
to be married to a
mediocre white man
right now because wow

dear one who disowned me

after decades of life together
I haven't seen you in six years

I had several poems written to/
about you but decided the ones

in my first book were enough
and I'm ready to let it go / I

will never not be sad that this
is our story but it doesn't sting

like it used to, just a dull ache
at times and weirdly I find that

saddest of all

I will always love you and
I hope you find peace

love
Marla

real quick before I let go

I do hold out hope that one
or more of your kids will

grow up to see the world as it
truly is and push back on what

they've been taught / I hope
you'll listen to them and love

them (and not the love that
feels like hate) / I hope you'll

open your heart and mind to
them instead of shutting them

out like you did me

deconstructing

picking up the pieces

you can't just deconstruct
you have to reconstruct

they like to tell me
don't worry / I am

I'm deconstructing my *beliefs*
and putting my *self* back together

here's to beautiful tales

"As we develop our awareness
about the barriers to belonging,

and our collective pursuit
for ultimate wholeness,

deconstruction involves
the work to

reclaim what gives life;
discard what does not;

and create beautiful tales."

—**Rohadi Nagassar**

the million-dollar question

but what do you
belieeeeeeeeeeve
now?

I don't know
and it doesn't really matter

believing or
not believing
Jesus died for my sins?

etc etc etc etc etc

doesn't change much
doesn't change me living
by a code of love

loving my neighbor
loving myself
loving loving loving

but can you be truly loving
without Jeeeeeeeesus?

watch me

the prodigy to prodigal pipeline

I used to be the very best
christian there ever was

the poster child
of poster children

now I'm on the playbill for
Backsliders & Heretics

what can I say?

I do some things
half-assed

but I guess this ain't
one of them

fruit salad

some christians think they have a
monopoly on the fruit of the spirit

but I know so many people
who exhibit way more

love
joy
peace
patience
goodness
kindness
gentleness
faithfulness
self-control

than they do and love people
because it's the right thing to do

and not because they want to
earn crowns in heaven

the idea that you can only bear fruit
with Jesus in your heart isn't true

some atheists follow your Jesus
better than you do

careening

I turned 40 and became a middle-
aged cliché, facing some of my

biggest fears / learned to drive a
moto in a foreign land, rode some

terrifyingly high/fast roller coasters
jumped off a 10-meter platform

diving board into the pool below / I
haven't roller-bladed down a hill but

I've deconstructed down a slippery
slope and it wasn't so bad / yeah you

might crash and get banged up, but
you'll be okay / a few scars, a broken

bone / you'll figure out the brakes and
it won't be so scary after all / steep

hills and big jumps might even be
something you seek out for fun someday

maybe

nothing to see here

I hold the knotted tangle of 347
delicate gold and silver chains

from my old jewelry box in my
hands / I will literally be here for

the rest of my damn life trying to
untangle them / is it really worth

my time and energy trying to save
two necklaces? / I've got so many

other things to do with my time

how about I just kiss the whole
clump, thank it for its service

(Marie Kondo-style) throw it out
with the filthy bathwater and

cut my losses?

well that explains a lot

there is something both bitter
and sweet about learning new

terminology for a thing I've
been doing, a way I've been

acting / like *spiritual bypassing*
where rather than work through

unpleasant emotions or real
world issues that make you

uncomfortable, you just slap on
a religious platitude and dismiss

the whole thing with a spiritual
phrase that explains it all away

I was so good at this for so long
and I'm digging up all the times

I used to do it so I can see it,
rebuke it, and help others get out

from under the heavy suffocating
weight of it too—and start to heal

[emphasis mine]

you're being just as dogmatic
about your new beliefs
as you were about your old ones
she told me
so that's just as bad

no, I'm being just as dogmatic
about being *wrong*
as I was about thinking I was *right*
there's a difference

I'm right I used to say
emphatically

and now?

I harmed people / I was wrong
emphatically

I'm going to stop the harm and make this right
emphatically

and I want you to stop too
emphatically

cheat sheet unavailable

please summarize all of
your beliefs she says

about every single thing
as succinctly as possible

so I can know how
I feel about you

no ma'am / I've been working
hard at this, sharing what I've

learned for over a decade and
you want to ignore the blood,

sweat, tears and swoop in
after the fact and say

hey, that's great but can
I just have the CliffsNotes?

you and I

you want to know
what my beliefs are
about the death, burial, and
resurrection of Jesus Christ
and how a person gets saved
from hell in the future

I want to know
when you're going to
stop doing harm and
inflicting hell on your
fellow humans right here
on earth right this minute

how it generally goes

heretic says something
christian doesn't like

christian demands that
heretic answer questions
"proving" her faith

I think that's a cop-out
let's flip it / christian can
answer some questions first

what do you believe
and why?

have you ever examined it closely?
and how?

what does "saved from my sins" mean?
like in words that mean actual things

I've never had to defend my
faith like you have, Marla
she says in frustration

yeah, no kidding

guess again

gotta love the folks who say *people*
just deconstruct so they can have sex

with whomever they want / I'm 47 and
have never had sex with someone I

wasn't married to / will I ever? / can't
say but I started deconstructing 10+

years ago so I'd say it's safe to assume
that horny wasn't my prime motivation

adjectivity

my friend David has a podcast
called *Graceful Atheist*
and he embodies the name so well

I'm not an atheist (not yet anyway)
but if I became one today and
started a podcast, I'd call it

Annoyed Atheist or
Disgruntled Atheist or
Pissed-Off Atheist

what would yours be called?

sticky falls

a river runs through a tropical forest / water
pours down big smooth cream-colored rocks

most waterfalls are slimy with algae / people
supposedly climb *up* Bua Thong Waterfalls

in Chiang Mai, Thailand / no thanks to slipping
on treacherous rocks, cracking my head / I'll just

look / but as I descend the stairs I watch people
climbing laughing chatting / these happy folks

are not professionals with fancy gear / they're
young/old/thin/fat / some hold kids or strap

them to their backs / solo climbers no older
than five / the rocks are grippable limestone

that algae can't adhere to / bare feet grip better
than flip-flops / you can hold on to ropes strung

from trees / cold clear water flows all around /
the climb is steep, your legs ache, but it's worth

it / the proof is in those up ahead on the not-so-
slippery-after-all slope having a marvelous time

a spong time coming

you might recall a haiku
in my previous book

where I read a few pages
of Rob Bell,

couldn't handle the
cognitive dissonance,

and threw it away

only to buy the book again later
read it, love it, rave about it

the very same thing happened with
Bishop John Shelby Spong recently

one book down,
lots to go

I find his work fascinating
and I'm kind of bummed
that it took me so spong

go (and come back) in peace

musician Derek Webb says he's *gotten*
very comfortable with a cycle of self-

sabotage / he's cool with shedding ⅓
of his audience annually, says, *you*

can't be mad at people who don't like
what you're doing now / be grateful

they were ever there / I'm going to
(try to) take this to heart / I've had a

lot of people leave my life but I also
periodically get messages from old

friends who say things like *I unfriended*
you four years ago because I didn't like

what you were saying about racism but
my eyes have been opened so hi again

well hello there and welcome back

ecdysis

I spot the snakeskin in the grass
and cautiously look around for the

creature that shed it / I don't see her
but ask out loud anyway

did it no longer fit you? / was it
old and worn out? / maybe full of

parasites? / I'll bet you feel so fresh
and renewed and ready to grow

I want this for me, shedding old
beliefs like rattlesnake skin, leaving

those dry crumbly things on the
ground, slithering on my merry way

in my shimmery new scales

deprogramming is a bitch

that's the poem

grab your trowel and brush

to figure things out and connect the
dots, we can't just move forward

we have to look back, we have to
dig, because a lot of it is buried

deep / digging for truth can be
uncomfortable, painful, even

world-shifting but whether we're
trying to heal or deconstruct our faith

or eradicate white supremacy, we
have to get to the bottom of it / and

speaking of bottoms, we *will* get sand
in our underwear and there will be

chafing but we'll do it anyway / there
are both skeletons and treasures down

there and we don't know which ones
are buried where and watch out for

landmines but otherwise it's great fun

you talk about deconstruction

like I took a wrecking ball
to a perfectly good house

on a whim for no reason

no the foundation is rotten
there are termites wreaking

havoc inside the walls and I'm
done covering up the holes

with pretty picture frames

palimpsest

I knocked down the house of cards
that was my shaky evangelical faith

and I'm building a new one with legos
that I can rearrange whenever I want

cut up some of the cards and made a tiny
coffee table book for my living room

hung three as wall art but painted over
the original designs in my personal style

used one as a welcome mat and put the
unsalvageable ones through the shredder

now scouring thrift stores for other decor
slowly making my new home my own

and loving the process—I'm in no rush

settle down

an old college acquaintance I haven't
talked to in 25 years sent me a FB msg

to ask me *where I've landed* / this is not
a new question and I find it boring

I haven't landed and no longer want to
I'll land in the ground when I die or

maybe I'll be cremated, ashes scattered
to the wind, in the sea, over the fields

so none of me lands in any one place at
all but enough of that talk / I'm hoping

to live for a long while and let me guess
you landed somewhere 25 years ago

and haven't budged since

loving myself

it's the enneagram 1 in me

I'm not a person who can
take the high road without

dealing with some shit that
happened on the low road

especially when it feels like I'm

smoothing over it
paving over it
pretending it
never happened

nope

guess who wins there?

the oppressor
the perpetrator
the colonizer

not on my watch

in-eff-able

they say God is ineffable—too great
to be described—and I was created

in their image which makes me
ineffable too / as in indescribably

great and also you probably do
not want to eff with me right now

benefit of the blah blah blah

how can I trust myself after I believed
all those lies? I yell into the void

you've always been able to trust yourself,
the void replies / they were the ones you

couldn't trust and they gaslighted you into
thinking it was you / it wasn't you / you

were good and thought other people were too
they weren't / aren't / not always anyway

when good people realize
their beliefs are harmful
they let them go

when bad people get told that
their beliefs are harmful
they double down

and yeah of course there's good
and bad in all of us but you know
what I mean

benediction for a single mom

I was on a Zoom call with several friends
and author Candice Benbow to talk about

her book, *Red Lip Theology*, which is
very much a love letter to her mama who

raised her alone (and had recently passed) /
her father chose not to be in her life / as a

new single mom it hit home hard / *no
matter how much my mother loved me,*

*what could I really be worth if my father
didn't?* she writes / her mama gave

everything she had to try to make up for
that lack / I do too / I told Candice this

and she spent the next few minutes filling up
my heart and soul (and my eyes with tears)

with beautiful anointed words about me
being a wonderful mother and more than

enough and I will never forget how she
made me feel for as long as I live

mantra

loving my neighbor as
myself means asking

what do I dream for me?

my dream for me is
supporting myself with

what I love (writing)

so that's my dream
for my neighbor too

if that's what they want

seeing god in me

"I've accepted that the whole of my life
will be a pilgrimage toward the sound
of the genuine in me.

This may sound troubling to
those who've been conditioned to believe
that our journey is to God and God alone,

but I say the two paths are one.

My journey to the truth of God
cannot be parsed from my journey
to the truth of who I am.

A fidelity to the true self
is a fidelity to the truth.

I won't apologize for this."

—Cole Arthur Riley

a moment of levity

I used to share a common language
with church people

now I share a common language
with activists and book lovers

and people who watch *Schitt's Creek* to
calm their mind every night before bed

people who enjoy *a little lunchtime chin wag*
to discuss *disgruntled pelicans* and *bashful clams*

and who understand why
today felt as hard as figuring out
how to fold in broken cheese

who know that *heavy salads*
might as well be casseroles and get that
now is not the time for well-intended placation

and when Moira tells Johnny
oh, we're past all that now
and Johnny says
I'm not quite past it, Moira

I'm with Johnny and it's why
I had to write this book

hard

the past three years have
taken a toll on me

on you too, I know

we have each lost things
that meant a lot to us

people we love
ways of life

and I am finding the
anger much easier

to put into words
than the pain

rhythms of bravery

I hope your bravery has rhythms, my
friend told me / *that build you up from*

the inside out as you share your courage
with the world / you deserve that

that's my wish-prayer for you too
my dear reader friend

new plan

throuple

I'm trying to be with
Jesus *and* all these
folks who are hurting

but if this threesome
doesn't work out
I'm choosing them

sign me up

"…prophets are those
who do not care
whether you are ready
to hear their message

They say it because
it has to be said
and because it is true."

—Richard Rohr

old and tired

Sal Khan says that *parts of
the system we now hold sacred...*

are in fact rather arbitrary and
tradition tends to cramp

imagination and he's referring
to the U.S. education system

but I can't help thinking of
white evangelical christianity

and how their sacred cows are
optional at best, harmful at worst

it's time to bring a little more love
and imagination to the equation

be right back

my favorite books are the
ones I have to put down to

google a question or look
up a vocabulary word or

write furiously on my laptop
or in a notebook because the

thoughts/ideas the author's
words have unleashed won't

stop coming/flowing and I
not-so-secretly hope you have

to put this book down a time
or two to create something

snowflakes

imagine thinking that because
I live in South Carolina

I don't know snow

when I lived in Ohio for 39 years
I've had ice on the insides of my

windows / I lived through an ice
storm that left us without power

for 2 weeks / I've shoveled 3 feet
of snow to get to my car / I've slid

on ice into a ditch on a country
road before cell phones and had

to walk a mile to call for help

so miss me with
you don't know snow

I was a conservative evangelical
christian for every minute of

those 39 years so I don't want to
hear any of that shit either

turn the other cheek?

only other cheek
I'm showing you
is this one back here

one-eighty

I'm still trying
my damnedest to
save people

it's just that saving people
looks a whole lot different
now

saving them
from

what I used to be

saving them
to

going forward

It is time to seek out the deepest
wisdom of those who have been
most silenced by the forces of history,

Valarie Kaur writes,

When I am in a place that begins *by*
recognizing indigenous peoples,
centers *black lives, and* leads *with*
women of color, I am in a place
of deep solidarity.

time to make myself bigger
and louder in spaces where
I've been stifled or silenced

while stepping down / holding back
listening and learning in spaces
where I've reigned supreme

i.e., topple the patriarchy and
follow women and queer people
of color leading the way

all ears

as a woman who spent years under
christian patriarchy I want to get free

but as a white cishet non-disabled
woman my freedom comes with

responsibility / I have to make damn
sure I'm not perpetuating homophobia

transphobia / white supremacy / ableism
or any other ism/phobia on my way up

and out / and only people from those
marginalized groups can tell me if I'm

doing that or not / it's my job to listen
then act, pivot, change, make right

look both ways

we can't distance ourselves from
white evangelicalism without

acknowledging our complicity in
white supremacy / we can't cross

from complementarianism to
feminism without seeing how not

just gender but race factors in / we
can't go from white evangelicalism

to deconstruction while ignoring
how it's different for Black folks

we can't cross the road without
watching the intersection

not the end of the world

*racists and antiracists can't build a new
world together*, Andre Henry says, *their*

visions are fundamentally incongruent
he doesn't believe in building bridges with

white supremacists, *even the benevolent
ones,* and neither do I / he invites us to walk

away from them and join people who are
trying to expand the global revolution for

racial justice and also to *embrace the
apocalypse* but warns that *once you are*

awake, you'll never go back to sleep / he
warns us that *we may not be able to bring*

*most of our loved ones through the
apocalypse with us* and I have found this

to be true but he does offer the hope of *a
post-apocalyptic community waiting for*

us on the other side / and I have found
that true as well / can't wait to share *more*

aspirations

forgiving my ex
and his family

is a literal line item
on my bucket list

not quiiite there yet
but writing poems is

super healing and
I can feel my heart

softening just a bit

uptight

I will never forget
the uncomfortable
sensation of always

having my
evangelical panties
in a wad

life without a
perpetual wedgie
feels so good

more

my secret

I wish I could write a book
how do you find the time?

well, instead of putting
all of my hot takes
in a tweet or a TikTok

I put all of my lukewarm
takes in a Google doc

I keep my mouth shut
and my fingers typing
and read and read
and listen and learn

and write and write
and rework and rework
and tweak and tweak
repeat repeat repeat repeat

and there you go
so so easy

except the total and
exact opposite of that

unbelieve / jaded / more

when you write a trilogy
of poetry books

it means that everything will
work out perfectly, right?

the shaky beginning (*check*)
the dark middle (*check*)

the happy happy ending (*?*)
(*please I really want this check*)

pass the sriracha

this book starts off pretty spicy
and ends on a much milder note

why?

the short answer:
writing calms me down

as I collected my thoughts,
I collected myself

but don't worry

there's still plenty of
spice on my shelves

the shortcut

the peaceful person you're seeing at
the end of the book is who I am now

largely unbothered but also committed
for life to the fight against injustice

a friend asked me yesterday how I'm
not just an absolute mess all the time

re: the ever-raging dumpster fire

I was for a long time / I was a wreck
and had to be / you can't go under it

around it / over it / gotta go through it

there's no shortcut / well there kind of
is / you can get there quicker, with less

wasted angst by learning from others

I'm still angry / but I don't use energy
to fuel my anger / my anger fuels *me*

all the way down to the root

we'll never find true peace
by pretending the bad never

happened

I'm not gonna stick my
head in the sand

unless I've also got a
shovel in my hand

and armed myself with
a good little plan

to get to the bottom of it all

hairesis / heresy

I married the first religion I met
I didn't really have a choice,

a say in the matter

it was presented to me when I was
a wee one as absolute only truth

and I was all the way in

now that I know better, I'm
taking my time to get to

know what other people
believe or don't believe

and more importantly
getting to know myself
and what I want

and mindfully choosing bit by bit

imagine my delight when
I found out that the Greek term
translated as "heresy" means

choice

freeeeeeeeee

they warned me that a life
without Christ would be empty

it's not

there is hope and joy and purpose
on the other side of
white evangelical christianity—

maybe christianity altogether

some people want me to reconstruct
some want me to become an atheist
some want me to forget church but cling to Jesus

I'm not getting married
to any one decision yet
and I may never

I can taste the freedom
and it's fucking delicious

my big dream

a world where every
human being is safe
to be their absolute
truest most authentic
self and is met with
joy and celebration
at every damn turn

worth every minute

the only thing I don't
love about writing books

is that it takes me hours and
hours and hours and days

and days and days and weeks
weeks weeks months months

months, sometimes years
to write one and then

you read it
in 55 minutes

also now that I've made
writing a book sound so
arduous (which it is)

I think it would be amazing
if you wrote one

I know not everybody needs to
tell their story in book form

but if you do, hit me up
I'd love to read it

glorified bibliography

okay yes you're on to me / I
admit it / you guessed my game

this book is just a trick to get
you to buy all the other books

I've mentioned in these pages
let me know if it worked

book curator is a title I take
seriously / I read books like

I'm going on a treasure hunt

when words fail

my friend, a Black man, read through a
rough draft of this book and offered this

poignant insight: *you quoted us and got
out of the way* / my heart leapt at his words

that was my deepest hope / *but maybe write
something about what friendship with us has*

meant to you, he said / *I love the way you
hold our words but maybe a poem* to *us?*

and I so badly want to do that but how?
all the mind-swirling words center *me*

thank you for...
what you've done for *me*
how you make *me* feel
how you've changed *my* life

can I honor *you* and leave *me* out of it?
am I asking the impossible?

maybe, probably, but I have to try

to my Black friends

you are beauty and joy and softness
you are humor and wit and brilliance

you are strength and dignity and love
you are grit and resilience and kindness

you are poem and story and song
you are hope and ambition and dreams

we are so different and so much the same
my world is better because you're in it

you don't need me to save you
and it's not your job to save me

I know that the world and history and
white supremacy and all of everything

conspires against our friendship and I want
to *thank you* for taking a chance on me

I hope with every bit of my soul that
being friends with me fills you up

like being friends with you fills me up
you are a blessing, a treasure, a gift

I love you

more: a sneak peek

more Black women
more womanist theology
more Indigenous wisdom
more honoring of mama earth
more exploration of other religions
more stargazing and cosmos and wonder
more awe and mystery
more digging into my past
more discovery of who I am
more dissolving of binaries
more god as queer
more words in other languages
more knowing and loving my body
more witches and heresy
more sexuality and sensuality
more divine female imagery
more healing and wholeness
more appreciation, not appropriation
more big wide expansive inclusive love

more more more more more

a _____ *poetic reckoning*

this book's subtitle
is missing an adjective
because none of them
felt just right

reckoning suggests
that something
has been settled,
a final account
has been given

but this is
just the beginning
more like

a *partial* poetic reckoning
a *precursory* poetic reckoning
an *inceptive* poetic reckoning
an *unfinished* poetic reckoning

bottom line: it's not over

when

you can't
say it all
say even less

so long, cover girl

poetry means letting go
of the compulsion to

cover every base
cover my ass

and just let what
I wrote be enough

appendix a: endnotes

8. fuck yeah! (D. L. Mayfield, "D.L. Recommends: Autistic Joy Edition," God Is My Special Interest)

12. hi, god / it's me, mara (Ruth 2:20)

13. dumpster fire (Audre Lorde, *The Cancer Journals*, 11)

14. like the shape of a book (Nafissa Thompson-Spires, *The 1619 Project*, 397)

15. holy anger liberates (Cole Arthur Riley, *This Here Flesh*, 107, 110, 118)

16. fierce love (Rev. Dr. Jacqui Lewis, *Fierce Love*, 204)

25. (purposely) lost in translation (Obery M. Hendricks, Jr., *Christians Against Christianity*, 39-40)

32. hiding god's word in your heart (John Taylor Gatto, *Weapons of Mass Instruction*, 17)

34. read the room (Richard Rohr, *Falling Upward*, 12)

43. Team Marla or Team Paul? (paraphrased from Philippians 3:5-6)

50. C+ god *(*Rob Bell, *Love Wins*, 98-108*)*

51. sorry about the hell (Rachel Held Evans, *Faith Unraveled*, 68-70)

54. shaking in its boots (Bishop John Shelby Spong, *Why Christianity Must Change or Die*, 4-5)

58. god's butt ("I Love You, Lord, and I Lift My Voice" by Laurie Klein, 1978)

71. I pity the fool (Elaine Pagels, *Why Religion?*, 103)

72. over / lord (Alice Walker, *The Same River Twice*, 148)

78. don't dance around disability (Keah Brown, *The Pretty One*, 55 and 59; Emily Ladau, *Demystifying Disability*, 17-18; Dr. Amy Kenny, *My Body Is Not a Prayer Request*, ix, 17)

80. no more disability metaphors (Dr. Amy Kenny, *My Body Is Not a Prayer Request*, 93-94; Emily Ladau, *Demystifying Disability*, 20)

81. prayerful perpetrators (Dr. Amy Kenny, *My Body Is Not a Prayer Request*, 1-3)

83. when did we see you? (Dr. Amy Kenny, *My Body Is Not a Prayer Request*, 33-34)

92. just a receptacle (Wilda Gafney, *Womanist Midrash*, 30)

97. sick of men (Renita Weems, *Just a Sister Away*, 89-90

102. exposed (Meghan Tschanz, episode 37 of *Broadening the Narrative* podcast)

104. it's mama god for me (Glennon Doyle, *Untamed*, 247)

105. The sacred Black feminine (Christena Cleveland, *God Is a Black Woman*, 17*)*

106. spice it up (t-shirt from Pete Enns from thebiblefornormalpeople.com)
107. she-god (Wilda Gafney, *Womanist Midrash*, 19-20)
108. from subservient to subversive (Sue Monk Kidd, *Dance of the Dissident Daughter*, 68)
111. pernicious (@jemartisby on Instagram, 11/02/22)
113. this twisted strand of christianity (Obery M. Hendricks, Jr., *Christians Against Christianity*, xi)
118. when in Rome (Howard Thurman, *Jesus and the Disinherited*, 22)
120. get your people (Andre Henry, *All the White Friends I Couldn't Keep*, 16)
121. so sick of this (Martin Luther King Jr., "Our Struggle," April 1956)
124. king jaded himself (Frederick Douglass, *Narrative of the Life of Frederick Douglass, An American Slave*, appendix)
126. scripture as chains (Howard Thurman, *Jesus and the Disinherited*, 20)
127. preach, sister (James H. Cone, *The Cross and the Lynching Tree*, 132)
130. refined palate (@PastorTrey05 on Twitter, 06/17/22)
131. not your business (Katie Cannon, *Katie's Canon*, 2)
132. we wrestle with it (Wilda Gafney, *Womanist Midrash*, 8)
134. dirty or clean? (Resmaa Menakem, *My Grandmother's Hands*, 19-20)
136. his ancestors' wildest dreams (Danté Stewart, *Shoutin' In the Fire*, 128-129)
142. the mythical melting pot (Karen González, *Beyond Welcome*, 17)
152. sit with this (Cole Arthur Riley, *This Here Flesh*, 98)
153. where privilege comes from (Rohadi Nagassar, *When We Belong*, 45)
154. vibranium (Tre Johnson, *Dreams of Wakanda*, 41 and 43)
162. creation stories matter (Robin Wall Kimmerer, *Braiding Sweetgrass*, 6-7)
166. thanksgiving address (Chief Jake Swamp, *Giving Thanks*)
170. we can easily afford this (Shannon Kearns, *In the Margins*, 21)
171. amen and then some (@theKevinGarcia_ on Twitter, 7/05/22)
175. get your Greek on (Kathy Baldock, *Walking the Bridgeless Canyon*, 236)
180. a god who cares about babies (Mitzi J. Smith, *Womanist Sass and Talk Back*, 92)
181. when you put it that way (Sam Harris, *Letter to a Christian Nation*, 38)
185. I did a little digging ("The Real Origins of the Religious Right," Randall Balmer, https://www.politico.com/magazine/story/2014/05/religious-right-real-origins-107133/)
191. me too (@RevJacquiLewis on Twitter, 05/03/22)
212. doubting is healthy (Zora Neale Hurston, *Their Eyes Were Watching God*, 21)
213. stretch marks (Alice Walker, *The Same River Twice*, 171)

215. the christian agnostic (Leslie D. Weatherhead, *The Christian Agnostic*, 63)
221. this should not be (@jspark3000 on Instagram, 06/21/22)
225. guarding my heart (Alice Walker, *The Same River Twice*, 43)
231. advantage: moi (Obery M. Hendricks Jr., *Christians Against Christianity*, xi)
236. can't see a bridge (Amy Tan, *Where the Past Begins*, 211)
245. here's to beautiful tales (Rohadi Nagassar, *When We Belong*, 76)
251. well that explains a lot ("spiritual bypassing" is a term coined by John Welwood in the 1980s)
260. go (and come back) in peace (episode 102 of the *Graceful Atheist* podcast)
273. seeing god in me (Cole Arthur Riley, *This Here Flesh*, 48)
274. a moment of levity (title and all italics are quotes from Dan Levy and Eugene Levy's *Schitt's Creek*)
279. sign me up (Richard Rohr, *Falling Upward*, 12)
280. old and tired (Sal Khan, *The One World Schoolhouse*, 62)
285. going forward (Valarie Kaur, *See No Stranger*, 287)
287. look both ways (Kimberlé Crenshaw coined the term "intersectionality" in 1989)
288. not the end of the world (Andre Henry, *All the White Friends I Couldn't Keep*, 151)
297. hairesis / heresy (Elaine Pagels, *Why Religion?*, 31)

appendix b: recommended books

antiracism
Shoutin' in the Fire, Danté Stewart
After Whiteness, Willie James Jennings
All the White Friends I Couldn't Keep, Andre Henry
Reading Black Books, Claude Atcho
My Grandmother's Hands, Resmaa Menakem
Doing Nothing Is No Longer an Option, Jenny Booth Potter

beyond evangelical christianity
Christians Against Christianity, Obery M. Hendricks
White Evangelical Racism, Anthea Butler
When We Belong, Rohadi Nagassar
Why Christianity Must Change or Die, John Shelby Spong
Christian Agnostic, Leslie D. Weatherhead
Why Religion?, Elaine Pagels

disability justice
My Body Is Not a Prayer Request, Dr. Amy Kenny
Demystifying Disability, Emily Ladau
The Pretty One, Keah Brown
Disability Visibility, edited by Alice Wong

a love ethic
Jesus and the Disinherited, Howard Thurman
See No Stranger, Valarie Kaur
Beyond Welcome, Karen González
Unruly Saint, D. L. Mayfield
Blessings for the Long Night, Jessica Kantrowitz

womanism (etc)
God Is a Black Woman, Christena Cleveland
Red Lip Theology, Candice Benbow
Katie's Canon, Katie Cannon
Just a Sister Away, Renita Weems
Womanist Sass and Talk Back, Mitzi Smith
Womanist Midrash, Wilda Gafney

beautiful books by Black women
This Here Flesh, Cole Arthur Riley
What Children Remember, Tasha Hunter
Read Until You Understand, Farah Jasmine Griffin
Peace Is a Practice, Morgan Harper Nichols
Fortune, Lisa Sharon Harper
Fierce Love, Rev. Dr. Jacqui Lewis
The Light of the World, Elizabeth Alexander
A Place to Belong, Amber O'Neal Johnston

Indigenous wisdom
For This Land, Vine Deloria Jr.
Becoming Rooted, Randy Woodley
Braiding Sweetgrass, Robin Wall Kimmerer
Poet Warrior, Joy Harjo
The Woman Who Watches Over the World, Linda Hogan
Gathering Moss, Robin Wall Kimmerer

LGBTQ+ theology
Walking the Bridgeless Canyon, Kathy Baldock
In the Margins, Shannon Kearns
Transforming, Austen Hartke

LGBTQ+ christian memoirs
Still Stace, Stacey Chomiak
Leather & Lace, Matt Bays
Love Him Well, Tyler Krumland
Intersexion, Cynthia Vacca Davis
Affirming, Sally Gary
She's My Dad, Jonathan S. Williams with Paula Stone Williams
How We Sleep at Night, Sara Cunningham
To Shake the Sleeping Self, Jedidiah Jenkins
My Gay Church Days, George Azar

deconstruction(ish) memoirs
As Familiar as Family, Nicki Pappas
Beyond Borders, Rachel Andersen
Women Rising, Meghan Tschanz
Charlie's Boy, Justin Charles Stauffer
Evangelical Anxiety, Charles Marsh

See Appendices A, B, and D in *unbelieve* for more books.

acknowledgements

I thank everybody in this book for coming.

—A. W., author and medium

Alice Walker wrote that brilliant blurb at the end of her classic *The Color Purple* as a thank you to all the characters in her novel. I too want to thank each "character" who wrote a book, tweeted a tweet, or said/did a thing that inspired the words in this book. THANK YOU.

Thank you, Amanda, Corrin, Deb, Diane, Gloria, Nicki, Paul, and Ruth for reading through a rough draft of this book and offering valuable feedback.

Thank you, Camille, Robert, Tasha, and Emerson, my sensitivity readers. This book is so much better because of your thoughtful, knowledgeable, experienced suggestions. Anything insensitive that remains is on me.

Thank you, Liv, for another gorgeous cover and making my sketches come to life. Thank you, Corrin, my Happiness Engineer, for single-handedly reviving my website—and so much more. Thank you, Paul, for your tireless labor of love on *unbelieve: the musical*.

Thank you to everyone who has read and shared *unbelieve*. My heart jumps for joy (and I do this weird happy handclap thing) when you take the time to tell me what she meant to you.

Thank you to my kids for being my whole entire heart.

Thank you to Nora, my laptop. Thank you, dining room table, living room couch, back deck glider, and bed (my four desks). Thank you, trees, for giving your lives so my words could be printed. Thank you, my gorgeous bookshelves and aaaaaaallll my books.

Thank you, orchids, ponytail palm, lucky bamboo, and all my other plant friends. Thank you, Bic pens, purple sticky notes, Aquaphor lip repair, book darts, Notes app on my iPhone, and 20-cent spiral notebooks from Target.

Oh, this could go on for years. I'll stop here. I LOVE YOU ALL!! See you in my next book!

about the author

Marla Taviano is into books, love, justice, globes, anti-racism, blue, gray, rainbows, and poems. She reads and writes for a living, wears her heart on her t-shirts, and is on a mission/quest/journey to live wholefarted (not a typo). She's the author of *unbelieve: poems on the journey to becoming a heretic*, and lives in South Carolina with her four freaking awesome kids. Find out more at marlataviano.com.

unbelieve

poems on the journey to becoming a heretic

Marla Taviano

"Marla's book of poetry is exactly the kind of expression that might poetically articulate your own journey."
David Hayward (aka NakedPastor), cartoonist and author of *Flip It Like This!*

"I love Marla's quest to absorb as much as she can about communities that are different from hers—and I am obsessed with her thoughtful book reviews. *Unbelieve* is her own story about her complicated journey with faith. I highly recommend it!"
Lisa Ling, journalist and host of CNN's "This Is Life with Lisa Ling"

"In *unbelieve*, Marla artfully and bravely gives all of us a front row seat to her own deconstruction while also welcoming us and helping us feel safe in our own wildernesses."
Matthew Paul Turner, NY Times bestselling author of *What Is God Like?*

"I'm just going to read a few poems a day. That's the lie I told myself when I started reading this poetry book. But I slurped the whole thing right up like a chai latte on a stressful day."
Amber O'Neal Johnston, author of *A Place to Belong*

"In *unbelieve*, Marla gives you permission to ask big questions and wrestle with big truths and not just continue to settle for a safe, status quo faith. Quite simply, *unbelieve* helps you . . . believe. In a bigger, bolder, and more authentic way."
Mandy Hale, New York Times bestselling author of *Turn Toward the Sun*

"One thing we can absolutely all agree on is that leaders in the American church have actively abused her people and have become increasingly antagonistic and isolated. Marla poetically makes the case, through humor and punchlines and snark and sharply devastating rhymes, that westernized Christian theology is to blame. You might disagree. But I hope you would be willing to hear Marla's case."

J. S. Park, hospital chaplain and author of *The Voices We Carry*

"These poems resonated as they met me where I am and where I have been. Marla asks the questions that too many have been taught should remain unspoken, inviting us along in her journey through an ever-evolving faith."

Patricia Taylor, writer and activist

"There are books that bring you comfort, books you return to time and time again, and books that make you feel like you are not alone. Somehow, Marla Taviano accomplished all three of these feats in her collection of narrative poetry, *unbelieve*."

Cara Meredith, author of *The Color of Life*